ISBN 0-8373-2641-9
C-2641   CAREER EXAMINATION SERIES

This is your PASSBOOK® for...

Safety Supervisor

Test Preparation Study Guide

Questions & Answers

NLC
NATIONAL LEARNING CORPORATION

Copyright © 2014 by

National Learning Corporation

212 Michael Drive, Syosset, New York 11791

All rights reserved, including the right of reproduction in whole or in part, in any form or by any means, electronic or mechanical, including photocopying, recording, or by any information storage and retrieval system, without permission in writing from the Publisher.

(516) 921-8888
(800) 645-6337
FAX: (516) 921-8743
www.passbooks.com
sales @ passbooks.com
info @ passbooks.com

PRINTED IN THE UNITED STATES OF AMERICA

PASSBOOK®
NOTICE

This book is SOLELY intended for, is sold ONLY to, and its use is RESTRICTED to *individual*, bona fide applicants or candidates who qualify by virtue of having seriously filed applications for appropriate license, certificate, professional and/or promotional advancement, higher school matriculation, scholarship, or other legitimate requirements of educational and/or governmental authorities.

This book is NOT intended for use, class instruction, tutoring, training, duplication, copying, reprinting, excerption, or adaptation, etc., by:

(1) Other publishers

(2) Proprietors and/or Instructors of "Coaching" and/or Preparatory Courses

(3) Personnel and/or Training Divisions of commercial, industrial, and governmental organizations

(4) Schools, colleges, or universities and/or their departments and staffs, including teachers and other personnel

(5) Testing Agencies or Bureaus

(6) Study groups which seek by the purchase of a single volume to copy and/or duplicate and/or adapt this material for use by the group as a whole without having purchased individual volumes for each of the members of the group

(7) Et al.

Such persons would be in violation of appropriate Federal and State statutes.

PROVISION OF LICENSING AGREEMENTS. — Recognized educational commercial, industrial, and governmental institutions and organizations, and others legitimately engaged in educational pursuits, including training, testing, and measurement activities, may address a request for a licensing agreement to the copyright owners, who will determine whether, and under what conditions, including fees and charges, the materials in this book may be used by them. In other words, a licensing facility exists for the legitimate use of the material in this book on other than an individual basis. However, it is asseverated and affirmed here that the material in this book *CANNOT* be used without the receipt of the express permission of such a licensing agreement from the Publishers.

NATIONAL LEARNING CORPORATION
212 Michael Drive
Syosset, New York 11791

Inquiries re licensing agreements should be addressed to:
The President
National Learning Corporation
212 Michael Drive
Syosset, New York 11791

PASSBOOK SERIES®

THE *PASSBOOK SERIES*® has been created to prepare applicants and candidates for the ultimate academic battlefield—the examination room.

At some time in our lives, each and every one of us may be required to take an examination—for validation, matriculation, admission, qualification, registration, certification, or licensure.

Based on the assumption that every applicant or candidate has met the basic formal educational standards, has taken the required number of courses, and read the necessary texts, the *PASSBOOK SERIES*® furnishes the one special preparation which may assure passing with confidence, instead of failing with insecurity. Examination questions—together with answers—are furnished as the basic vehicle for study so that the mysteries of the examination and its compounding difficulties may be eliminated or diminished by a sure method.

This book is meant to help you pass your examination provided that you qualify and are serious in your objective.

The entire field is reviewed through the huge store of content information which is succinctly presented through a provocative and challenging approach—the question-and-answer method.

A climate of success is established by furnishing the correct answers at the end of each test.

You soon learn to recognize types of questions, forms of questions, and patterns of questioning. You may even begin to anticipate expected outcomes.

You perceive that many questions are repeated or adapted so that you gain acute insights, which may enable you to score many sure points.

You learn how to confront new questions, or types of questions, and to attack them confidently and work out the correct answers.

You note objectives and emphases, and recognize pitfalls and dangers, so that you may make positive educational adjustments.

Moreover, you are kept fully informed in relation to new concepts, methods, practices, and directions in the field.

You discover that you are actually taking the examination all the time: you are preparing for the examination by "taking" an examination, not by reading extraneous and/or supererogatory textbooks.

In short, this PASSBOOK®, used directedly, should be an important factor in helping you to pass your test.

SAFETY SUPERVISOR

DUTIES
Develops, organizes and implements a comprehensive safety program for a governmental agency, and is responsible for maintaining Federal, State and local safety and health standards. Conducts safety awareness training programs for County personnel; disseminates educational materials to promote safe conditions. Inspects buildings and grounds, identifies hazards and takes action to rectify them. Performs related work as required.

SCOPE OF THE EXAMINATION
The written test will be designed to test for knowledge, skills, and/or abilities in such areas as:
1. Preparing written material;
2. Understanding and interpreting written material;
3. Supervision;
4. Inspection and investigative techniques;
5. Accident prevention and control;
6. Statutory and regulatory requirements relating to occupational health and safety, and building safety; and
7. Administering, supervising and evaluating training programs.

HOW TO TAKE A TEST

I. YOU MUST PASS AN EXAMINATION

A. *WHAT EVERY CANDIDATE SHOULD KNOW*

Examination applicants often ask us for help in preparing for the written test. What can I study in advance? What kinds of questions will be asked? How will the test be given? How will the papers be graded?

As an applicant for a civil service examination, you may be wondering about some of these things. Our purpose here is to suggest effective methods of advance study and to describe civil service examinations.

Your chances for success on this examination can be increased if you know how to prepare. Those "pre-examination jitters" can be reduced if you know what to expect. You can even experience an adventure in good citizenship if you know why civil service exams are given.

B. *WHY ARE CIVIL SERVICE EXAMINATIONS GIVEN?*

Civil service examinations are important to you in two ways. As a citizen, you want public jobs filled by employees who know how to do their work. As a job seeker, you want a fair chance to compete for that job on an equal footing with other candidates. The best-known means of accomplishing this two-fold goal is the competitive examination.

Exams are widely publicized throughout the nation. They may be administered for jobs in federal, state, city, municipal, town or village governments or agencies.

Any citizen may apply, with some limitations, such as the age or residence of applicants. Your experience and education may be reviewed to see whether you meet the requirements for the particular examination. When these requirements exist, they are reasonable and applied consistently to all applicants. Thus, a competitive examination may cause you some uneasiness now, but it is your privilege and safeguard.

C. *HOW ARE CIVIL SERVICE EXAMS DEVELOPED?*

Examinations are carefully written by trained technicians who are specialists in the field known as "psychological measurement," in consultation with recognized authorities in the field of work that the test will cover. These experts recommend the subject matter areas or skills to be tested; only those knowledges or skills important to your success on the job are included. The most reliable books and source materials available are used as references. Together, the experts and technicians judge the difficulty level of the questions.

Test technicians know how to phrase questions so that the problem is clearly stated. Their ethics do not permit "trick" or "catch" questions. Questions may have been tried out on sample groups, or subjected to statistical analysis, to determine their usefulness.

Written tests are often used in combination with performance tests, ratings of training and experience, and oral interviews. All of these measures combine to form the best-known means of finding the right person for the right job.

II. HOW TO PASS THE WRITTEN TEST

A. NATURE OF THE EXAMINATION

To prepare intelligently for civil service examinations, you should know how they differ from school examinations you have taken. In school you were assigned certain definite pages to read or subjects to cover. The examination questions were quite detailed and usually emphasized memory. Civil service exams, on the other hand, try to discover your present ability to perform the duties of a position, plus your potentiality to learn these duties. In other words, a civil service exam attempts to predict how successful you will be. Questions cover such a broad area that they cannot be as minute and detailed as school exam questions.

In the public service similar kinds of work, or positions, are grouped together in one "class." This process is known as *position-classification*. All the positions in a class are paid according to the salary range for that class. One class title covers all of these positions, and they are all tested by the same examination.

B. FOUR BASIC STEPS

1) Study the announcement

How, then, can you know what subjects to study? Our best answer is: "Learn as much as possible about the class of positions for which you've applied." The exam will test the knowledge, skills and abilities needed to do the work.

Your most valuable source of information about the position you want is the official exam announcement. This announcement lists the training and experience qualifications. Check these standards and apply only if you come reasonably close to meeting them.

The brief description of the position in the examination announcement offers some clues to the subjects which will be tested. Think about the job itself. Review the duties in your mind. Can you perform them, or are there some in which you are rusty? Fill in the blank spots in your preparation.

Many jurisdictions preview the written test in the exam announcement by including a section called "Knowledge and Abilities Required," "Scope of the Examination," or some similar heading. Here you will find out specifically what fields will be tested.

2) Review your own background

Once you learn in general what the position is all about, and what you need to know to do the work, ask yourself which subjects you already know fairly well and which need improvement. You may wonder whether to concentrate on improving your strong areas or on building some background in your fields of weakness. When the announcement has specified "some knowledge" or "considerable knowledge," or has used adjectives like "beginning principles of..." or "advanced ... methods," you can get a clue as to the number and difficulty of questions to be asked in any given field. More questions, and hence broader coverage, would be included for those subjects which are more important in the work. Now weigh your strengths and weaknesses against the job requirements and prepare accordingly.

3) Determine the level of the position

Another way to tell how intensively you should prepare is to understand the level of the job for which you are applying. Is it the entering level? In other words, is this the position in which beginners in a field of work are hired? Or is it an intermediate or advanced level? Sometimes this is indicated by such words as "Junior" or "Senior" in the class title. Other jurisdictions use Roman numerals to designate the level – Clerk I, Clerk II, for example. The word "Supervisor" sometimes appears in the title. If the level is not indicated by the title, check the description of duties. Will you be working under very close supervision, or will you have responsibility for independent decisions in this work?

4) Choose appropriate study materials

Now that you know the subjects to be examined and the relative amount of each subject to be covered, you can choose suitable study materials. For beginning level jobs, or even advanced ones, if you have a pronounced weakness in some aspect of your training, read a modern, standard textbook in that field. Be sure it is up to date and has general coverage. Such books are normally available at your library, and the librarian will be glad to help you locate one. For entry-level positions, questions of appropriate difficulty are chosen – neither highly advanced questions, nor those too simple. Such questions require careful thought but not advanced training.

If the position for which you are applying is technical or advanced, you will read more advanced, specialized material. If you are already familiar with the basic principles of your field, elementary textbooks would waste your time. Concentrate on advanced textbooks and technical periodicals. Think through the concepts and review difficult problems in your field.

These are all general sources. You can get more ideas on your own initiative, following these leads. For example, training manuals and publications of the government agency which employs workers in your field can be useful, particularly for technical and professional positions. A letter or visit to the government department involved may result in more specific study suggestions, and certainly will provide you with a more definite idea of the exact nature of the position you are seeking.

III. KINDS OF TESTS

Tests are used for purposes other than measuring knowledge and ability to perform specified duties. For some positions, it is equally important to test ability to make adjustments to new situations or to profit from training. In others, basic mental abilities not dependent on information are essential. Questions which test these things may not appear as pertinent to the duties of the position as those which test for knowledge and information. Yet they are often highly important parts of a fair examination. For very general questions, it is almost impossible to help you direct your study efforts. What we can do is to point out some of the more common of these general abilities needed in public service positions and describe some typical questions.

1) General information

Broad, general information has been found useful for predicting job success in some kinds of work. This is tested in a variety of ways, from vocabulary lists to questions about current events. Basic background in some field of work, such as sociology or economics, may be sampled in a group of questions. Often these are principles which have become familiar to most persons through exposure rather than through formal training. It is difficult to advise you how to study for these questions; being alert to the world around you is our best suggestion.

2) Verbal ability
An example of an ability needed in many positions is verbal or language ability. Verbal ability is, in brief, the ability to use and understand words. Vocabulary and grammar tests are typical measures of this ability. Reading comprehension or paragraph interpretation questions are common in many kinds of civil service tests. You are given a paragraph of written material and asked to find its central meaning.

3) Numerical ability
Number skills can be tested by the familiar arithmetic problem, by checking paired lists of numbers to see which are alike and which are different, or by interpreting charts and graphs. In the latter test, a graph may be printed in the test booklet which you are asked to use as the basis for answering questions.

4) Observation
A popular test for law-enforcement positions is the observation test. A picture is shown to you for several minutes, then taken away. Questions about the picture test your ability to observe both details and larger elements.

5) Following directions
In many positions in the public service, the employee must be able to carry out written instructions dependably and accurately. You may be given a chart with several columns, each column listing a variety of information. The questions require you to carry out directions involving the information given in the chart.

6) Skills and aptitudes
Performance tests effectively measure some manual skills and aptitudes. When the skill is one in which you are trained, such as typing or shorthand, you can practice. These tests are often very much like those given in business school or high school courses. For many of the other skills and aptitudes, however, no short-time preparation can be made. Skills and abilities natural to you or that you have developed throughout your lifetime are being tested.

Many of the general questions just described provide all the data needed to answer the questions and ask you to use your reasoning ability to find the answers. Your best preparation for these tests, as well as for tests of facts and ideas, is to be at your physical and mental best. You, no doubt, have your own methods of getting into an exam-taking mood and keeping "in shape." The next section lists some ideas on this subject.

IV. KINDS OF QUESTIONS

Only rarely is the "essay" question, which you answer in narrative form, used in civil service tests. Civil service tests are usually of the short-answer type. Full instructions for answering these questions will be given to you at the examination. But in case this is your first experience with short-answer questions and separate answer sheets, here is what you need to know:

1) Multiple-choice Questions

Most popular of the short-answer questions is the "multiple choice" or "best answer" question. It can be used, for example, to test for factual knowledge, ability to solve problems or judgment in meeting situations found at work.

A multiple-choice question is normally one of three types—

- It can begin with an incomplete statement followed by several possible endings. You are to find the one ending which *best* completes the statement, although some of the others may not be entirely wrong.
- It can also be a complete statement in the form of a question which is answered by choosing one of the statements listed.
- It can be in the form of a problem – again you select the best answer.

Here is an example of a multiple-choice question with a discussion which should give you some clues as to the method for choosing the right answer:

When an employee has a complaint about his assignment, the action which will *best* help him overcome his difficulty is to

    A. discuss his difficulty with his coworkers
    B. take the problem to the head of the organization
    C. take the problem to the person who gave him the assignment
    D. say nothing to anyone about his complaint

In answering this question, you should study each of the choices to find which is best. Consider choice "A" – Certainly an employee may discuss his complaint with fellow employees, but no change or improvement can result, and the complaint remains unresolved. Choice "B" is a poor choice since the head of the organization probably does not know what assignment you have been given, and taking your problem to him is known as "going over the head" of the supervisor. The supervisor, or person who made the assignment, is the person who can clarify it or correct any injustice. Choice "C" is, therefore, correct. To say nothing, as in choice "D," is unwise. Supervisors have and interest in knowing the problems employees are facing, and the employee is seeking a solution to his problem.

2) True/False Questions

The "true/false" or "right/wrong" form of question is sometimes used. Here a complete statement is given. Your job is to decide whether the statement is right or wrong.

SAMPLE: A person-to-person long-distance telephone call costs less than a station-to-station call to the same city.

This statement is wrong, or false, since person-to-person calls are more expensive.

This is not a complete list of all possible question forms, although most of the others are variations of these common types. You will always get complete directions for answering questions. Be sure you understand *how* to mark your answers – ask questions until you do.

V. RECORDING YOUR ANSWERS

For an examination with very few applicants, you may be told to record your answers in the test booklet itself. Separate answer sheets are much more common. If this separate answer sheet is to be scored by machine – and this is often the case – it is highly important that you mark your answers correctly in order to get credit.

An electric scoring machine is often used in civil service offices because of the speed with which papers can be scored. Machine-scored answer sheets must be marked with a pencil, which will be given to you. This pencil has a high graphite content which responds to the electric scoring machine. As a matter of fact, stray dots may register as answers, so do not let your pencil rest on the answer sheet while you are pondering the correct answer. Also, if your pencil lead breaks or is otherwise defective, ask for another.

Since the answer sheet will be dropped in a slot in the scoring machine, be careful not to bend the corners or get the paper crumpled.

The answer sheet normally has five vertical columns of numbers, with 30 numbers to a column. These numbers correspond to the question numbers in your test booklet. After each number, going across the page are four or five pairs of dotted lines. These short dotted lines have small letters or numbers above them. The first two pairs may also have a "T" or "F" above the letters. This indicates that the first two pairs only are to be used if the questions are of the true-false type. If the questions are multiple choice, disregard the "T" and "F" and pay attention only to the small letters or numbers.

Answer your questions in the manner of the sample that follows:

32. The largest city in the United States is
   A. Washington, D.C.
   B. New York City
   C. Chicago
   D. Detroit
   E. San Francisco

1) Choose the answer you think is best. (New York City is the largest, so "B" is correct.)
2) Find the row of dotted lines numbered the same as the question you are answering. (Find row number 32)
3) Find the pair of dotted lines corresponding to the answer. (Find the pair of lines under the mark "B.")
4) Make a solid black mark between the dotted lines.

VI. BEFORE THE TEST

Common sense will help you find procedures to follow to get ready for an examination. Too many of us, however, overlook these sensible measures. Indeed, nervousness and fatigue have been found to be the most serious reasons why applicants fail to do their best on civil service tests. Here is a list of reminders:

- Begin your preparation early – Don't wait until the last minute to go scurrying around for books and materials or to find out what the position is all about.
- Prepare continuously – An hour a night for a week is better than an all-night cram session. This has been definitely established. What is more, a night a

week for a month will return better dividends than crowding your study into a shorter period of time.
- Locate the place of the exam – You have been sent a notice telling you when and where to report for the examination. If the location is in a different town or otherwise unfamiliar to you, it would be well to inquire the best route and learn something about the building.
- Relax the night before the test – Allow your mind to rest. Do not study at all that night. Plan some mild recreation or diversion; then go to bed early and get a good night's sleep.
- Get up early enough to make a leisurely trip to the place for the test – This way unforeseen events, traffic snarls, unfamiliar buildings, etc. will not upset you.
- Dress comfortably – A written test is not a fashion show. You will be known by number and not by name, so wear something comfortable.
- Leave excess paraphernalia at home – Shopping bags and odd bundles will get in your way. You need bring only the items mentioned in the official notice you received; usually everything you need is provided. Do not bring reference books to the exam. They will only confuse those last minutes and be taken away from you when in the test room.
- Arrive somewhat ahead of time – If because of transportation schedules you must get there very early, bring a newspaper or magazine to take your mind off yourself while waiting.
- Locate the examination room – When you have found the proper room, you will be directed to the seat or part of the room where you will sit. Sometimes you are given a sheet of instructions to read while you are waiting. Do not fill out any forms until you are told to do so; just read them and be prepared.
- Relax and prepare to listen to the instructions
- If you have any physical problem that may keep you from doing your best, be sure to tell the test administrator. If you are sick or in poor health, you really cannot do your best on the exam. You can come back and take the test some other time.

VII. AT THE TEST

The day of the test is here and you have the test booklet in your hand. The temptation to get going is very strong. Caution! There is more to success than knowing the right answers. You must know how to identify your papers and understand variations in the type of short-answer question used in this particular examination. Follow these suggestions for maximum results from your efforts:

1) Cooperate with the monitor

The test administrator has a duty to create a situation in which you can be as much at ease as possible. He will give instructions, tell you when to begin, check to see that you are marking your answer sheet correctly, and so on. He is not there to guard you, although he will see that your competitors do not take unfair advantage. He wants to help you do your best.

2) Listen to all instructions

Don't jump the gun! Wait until you understand all directions. In most civil service tests you get more time than you need to answer the questions. So don't be in a hurry.

Read each word of instructions until you clearly understand the meaning. Study the examples, listen to all announcements and follow directions. Ask questions if you do not understand what to do.

3) Identify your papers
Civil service exams are usually identified by number only. You will be assigned a number; you must not put your name on your test papers. Be sure to copy your number correctly. Since more than one exam may be given, copy your exact examination title.

4) Plan your time
Unless you are told that a test is a "speed" or "rate of work" test, speed itself is usually not important. Time enough to answer all the questions will be provided, but this does not mean that you have all day. An overall time limit has been set. Divide the total time (in minutes) by the number of questions to determine the approximate time you have for each question.

5) Do not linger over difficult questions
If you come across a difficult question, mark it with a paper clip (useful to have along) and come back to it when you have been through the booklet. One caution if you do this – be sure to skip a number on your answer sheet as well. Check often to be sure that you have not lost your place and that you are marking in the row numbered the same as the question you are answering.

6) Read the questions
Be sure you know what the question asks! Many capable people are unsuccessful because they failed to *read* the questions correctly.

7) Answer all questions
Unless you have been instructed that a penalty will be deducted for incorrect answers, it is better to guess than to omit a question.

8) Speed tests
It is often better NOT to guess on speed tests. It has been found that on timed tests people are tempted to spend the last few seconds before time is called in marking answers at random – without even reading them – in the hope of picking up a few extra points. To discourage this practice, the instructions may warn you that your score will be "corrected" for guessing. That is, a penalty will be applied. The incorrect answers will be deducted from the correct ones, or some other penalty formula will be used.

9) Review your answers
If you finish before time is called, go back to the questions you guessed or omitted to give them further thought. Review other answers if you have time.

10) Return your test materials
If you are ready to leave before others have finished or time is called, take ALL your materials to the monitor and leave quietly. Never take any test material with you. The monitor can discover whose papers are not complete, and taking a test booklet may be grounds for disqualification.

VIII. EXAMINATION TECHNIQUES

1) Read the general instructions carefully. These are usually printed on the first page of the exam booklet. As a rule, these instructions refer to the timing of the examination; the fact that you should not start work until the signal and must stop work at a signal, etc. If there are any *special* instructions, such as a choice of questions to be answered, make sure that you note this instruction carefully.

2) When you are ready to start work on the examination, that is as soon as the signal has been given, read the instructions to each question booklet, underline any key words or phrases, such as *least, best, outline, describe* and the like. In this way you will tend to answer as requested rather than discover on reviewing your paper that you *listed without describing*, that you selected the *worst* choice rather than the *best* choice, etc.

3) If the examination is of the objective or multiple-choice type – that is, each question will also give a series of possible answers: A, B, C or D, and you are called upon to select the best answer and write the letter next to that answer on your answer paper – it is advisable to start answering each question in turn. There may be anywhere from 50 to 100 such questions in the three or four hours allotted and you can see how much time would be taken if you read through all the questions before beginning to answer any. Furthermore, if you come across a question or group of questions which you know would be difficult to answer, it would undoubtedly affect your handling of all the other questions.

4) If the examination is of the essay type and contains but a few questions, it is a moot point as to whether you should read all the questions before starting to answer any one. Of course, if you are given a choice – say five out of seven and the like – then it is essential to read all the questions so you can eliminate the two that are most difficult. If, however, you are asked to answer all the questions, there may be danger in trying to answer the easiest one first because you may find that you will spend too much time on it. The best technique is to answer the first question, then proceed to the second, etc.

5) Time your answers. Before the exam begins, write down the time it started, then add the time allowed for the examination and write down the time it must be completed, then divide the time available somewhat as follows:
   - If 3-1/2 hours are allowed, that would be 210 minutes. If you have 80 objective-type questions, that would be an average of 2-1/2 minutes per question. Allow yourself no more than 2 minutes per question, or a total of 160 minutes, which will permit about 50 minutes to review.
   - If for the time allotment of 210 minutes there are 7 essay questions to answer, that would average about 30 minutes a question. Give yourself only 25 minutes per question so that you have about 35 minutes to review.

6) The most important instruction is to *read each question* and make sure you know what is wanted. The second most important instruction is to *time yourself properly* so that you answer every question. The third most

important instruction is to *answer every question*. Guess if you have to but include something for each question. Remember that you will receive no credit for a blank and will probably receive some credit if you write something in answer to an essay question. If you guess a letter – say "B" for a multiple-choice question – you may have guessed right. If you leave a blank as an answer to a multiple-choice question, the examiners may respect your feelings but it will not add a point to your score. Some exams may penalize you for wrong answers, so in such cases *only*, you may not want to guess unless you have some basis for your answer.

7) Suggestions
   a. Objective-type questions
      1. Examine the question booklet for proper sequence of pages and questions
      2. Read all instructions carefully
      3. Skip any question which seems too difficult; return to it after all other questions have been answered
      4. Apportion your time properly; do not spend too much time on any single question or group of questions
      5. Note and underline key words – *all, most, fewest, least, best, worst, same, opposite*, etc.
      6. Pay particular attention to negatives
      7. Note unusual option, e.g., unduly long, short, complex, different or similar in content to the body of the question
      8. Observe the use of "hedging" words – *probably, may, most likely*, etc.
      9. Make sure that your answer is put next to the same number as the question
      10. Do not second-guess unless you have good reason to believe the second answer is definitely more correct
      11. Cross out original answer if you decide another answer is more accurate; do not erase until you are ready to hand your paper in
      12. Answer all questions; guess unless instructed otherwise
      13. Leave time for review

   b. Essay questions
      1. Read each question carefully
      2. Determine exactly what is wanted. Underline key words or phrases.
      3. Decide on outline or paragraph answer
      4. Include many different points and elements unless asked to develop any one or two points or elements
      5. Show impartiality by giving pros and cons unless directed to select one side only
      6. Make and write down any assumptions you find necessary to answer the questions
      7. Watch your English, grammar, punctuation and choice of words
      8. Time your answers; don't crowd material

8) Answering the essay question

Most essay questions can be answered by framing the specific response around several key words or ideas. Here are a few such key words or ideas:

M's: manpower, materials, methods, money, management
P's: purpose, program, policy, plan, procedure, practice, problems, pitfalls, personnel, public relations

  a. Six basic steps in handling problems:
     1. Preliminary plan and background development
     2. Collect information, data and facts
     3. Analyze and interpret information, data and facts
     4. Analyze and develop solutions as well as make recommendations
     5. Prepare report and sell recommendations
     6. Install recommendations and follow up effectiveness

  b. Pitfalls to avoid
     1. *Taking things for granted* – A statement of the situation does not necessarily imply that each of the elements is necessarily true; for example, a complaint may be invalid and biased so that all that can be taken for granted is that a complaint has been registered
     2. *Considering only one side of a situation* – Wherever possible, indicate several alternatives and then point out the reasons you selected the best one
     3. *Failing to indicate follow up* – Whenever your answer indicates action on your part, make certain that you will take proper follow-up action to see how successful your recommendations, procedures or actions turn out to be
     4. *Taking too long in answering any single question* – Remember to time your answers properly

IX. AFTER THE TEST

Scoring procedures differ in detail among civil service jurisdictions although the general principles are the same. Whether the papers are hand-scored or graded by machine we have described, they are nearly always graded by number. That is, the person who marks the paper knows only the number – never the name – of the applicant. Not until all the papers have been graded will they be matched with names. If other tests, such as training and experience or oral interview ratings have been given, scores will be combined. Different parts of the examination usually have different weights. For example, the written test might count 60 percent of the final grade, and a rating of training and experience 40 percent. In many jurisdictions, veterans will have a certain number of points added to their grades.

After the final grade has been determined, the names are placed in grade order and an eligible list is established. There are various methods for resolving ties between those who get the same final grade – probably the most common is to place first the name of the person whose application was received first. Job offers are made from the eligible list in the order the names appear on it. You will be notified of your grade and your rank as soon as all these computations have been made. This will be done as rapidly as possible.

People who are found to meet the requirements in the announcement are called "eligibles." Their names are put on a list of eligible candidates. An eligible's chances of getting a job depend on how high he stands on this list and how fast agencies are filling jobs from the list.

When a job is to be filled from a list of eligibles, the agency asks for the names of people on the list of eligibles for that job. When the civil service commission receives this request, it sends to the agency the names of the three people highest on this list. Or, if the job to be filled has specialized requirements, the office sends the agency the names of the top three persons who meet these requirements from the general list.

The appointing officer makes a choice from among the three people whose names were sent to him. If the selected person accepts the appointment, the names of the others are put back on the list to be considered for future openings.

That is the rule in hiring from all kinds of eligible lists, whether they are for typist, carpenter, chemist, or something else. For every vacancy, the appointing officer has his choice of any one of the top three eligibles on the list. This explains why the person whose name is on top of the list sometimes does not get an appointment when some of the persons lower on the list do. If the appointing officer chooses the second or third eligible, the No. 1 eligible does not get a job at once, but stays on the list until he is appointed or the list is terminated.

X. HOW TO PASS THE INTERVIEW TEST

The examination for which you applied requires an oral interview test. You have already taken the written test and you are now being called for the interview test – the final part of the formal examination.

You may think that it is not possible to prepare for an interview test and that there are no procedures to follow during an interview. Our purpose is to point out some things you can do in advance that will help you and some good rules to follow and pitfalls to avoid while you are being interviewed.

What is an interview supposed to test?

The written examination is designed to test the technical knowledge and competence of the candidate; the oral is designed to evaluate intangible qualities, not readily measured otherwise, and to establish a list showing the relative fitness of each candidate – as measured against his competitors – for the position sought. Scoring is not on the basis of "right" and "wrong," but on a sliding scale of values ranging from "not passable" to "outstanding." As a matter of fact, it is possible to achieve a relatively low score without a single "incorrect" answer because of evident weakness in the qualities being measured.

Occasionally, an examination may consist entirely of an oral test – either an individual or a group oral. In such cases, information is sought concerning the technical knowledges and abilities of the candidate, since there has been no written examination for this purpose. More commonly, however, an oral test is used to supplement a written examination.

Who conducts interviews?

The composition of oral boards varies among different jurisdictions. In nearly all, a representative of the personnel department serves as chairman. One of the members of the board may be a representative of the department in which the candidate would work. In some cases, "outside experts" are used, and, frequently, a businessman or some other representative of the general public is asked to serve. Labor and management or other special groups may be represented. The aim is to secure the services of experts in the appropriate field.

However the board is composed, it is a good idea (and not at all improper or unethical) to ascertain in advance of the interview who the members are and what groups they represent. When you are introduced to them, you will have some idea of their backgrounds and interests, and at least you will not stutter and stammer over their names.

What should be done before the interview?
While knowledge about the board members is useful and takes some of the surprise element out of the interview, there is other preparation which is more substantive. It *is* possible to prepare for an oral interview – in several ways:

1) Keep a copy of your application and review it carefully before the interview
This may be the only document before the oral board, and the starting point of the interview. Know what education and experience you have listed there, and the sequence and dates of all of it. Sometimes the board will ask you to review the highlights of your experience for them; you should not have to hem and haw doing it.

2) Study the class specification and the examination announcement
Usually, the oral board has one or both of these to guide them. The qualities, characteristics or knowledges required by the position sought are stated in these documents. They offer valuable clues as to the nature of the oral interview. For example, if the job involves supervisory responsibilities, the announcement will usually indicate that knowledge of modern supervisory methods and the qualifications of the candidate as a supervisor will be tested. If so, you can expect such questions, frequently in the form of a hypothetical situation which you are expected to solve. NEVER go into an oral without knowledge of the duties and responsibilities of the job you seek.

3) Think through each qualification required
Try to visualize the kind of questions you would ask if you were a board member. How well could you answer them? Try especially to appraise your own knowledge and background in each area, *measured against the job sought*, and identify any areas in which you are weak. Be critical and realistic – do not flatter yourself.

4) Do some general reading in areas in which you feel you may be weak
For example, if the job involves supervision and your past experience has NOT, some general reading in supervisory methods and practices, particularly in the field of human relations, might be useful. Do NOT study agency procedures or detailed manuals. The oral board will be testing your understanding and capacity, not your memory.

5) Get a good night's sleep and watch your general health and mental attitude
You will want a clear head at the interview. Take care of a cold or any other minor ailment, and of course, no hangovers.

What should be done on the day of the interview?
Now comes the day of the interview itself. Give yourself plenty of time to get there. Plan to arrive somewhat ahead of the scheduled time, particularly if your appointment is in the fore part of the day. If a previous candidate fails to appear, the board might be ready for you a bit early. By early afternoon an oral board is almost invariably behind schedule if there are many candidates, and you may have to wait.

Take along a book or magazine to read, or your application to review, but leave any extraneous material in the waiting room when you go in for your interview. In any event, relax and compose yourself.

The matter of dress is important. The board is forming impressions about you – from your experience, your manners, your attitude, and your appearance. Give your personal appearance careful attention. Dress your best, but not your flashiest. Choose conservative, appropriate clothing, and be sure it is immaculate. This is a business interview, and your appearance should indicate that you regard it as such. Besides, being well groomed and properly dressed will help boost your confidence.

Sooner or later, someone will call your name and escort you into the interview room. *This is it.* From here on you are on your own. It is too late for any more preparation. But remember, you asked for this opportunity to prove your fitness, and you are here because your request was granted.

What happens when you go in?

The usual sequence of events will be as follows: The clerk (who is often the board stenographer) will introduce you to the chairman of the oral board, who will introduce you to the other members of the board. Acknowledge the introductions before you sit down. Do not be surprised if you find a microphone facing you or a stenotypist sitting by. Oral interviews are usually recorded in the event of an appeal or other review.

Usually the chairman of the board will open the interview by reviewing the highlights of your education and work experience from your application – primarily for the benefit of the other members of the board, as well as to get the material into the record. Do not interrupt or comment unless there is an error or significant misinterpretation; if that is the case, do not hesitate. But do not quibble about insignificant matters. Also, he will usually ask you some question about your education, experience or your present job – partly to get you to start talking and to establish the interviewing "rapport." He may start the actual questioning, or turn it over to one of the other members. Frequently, each member undertakes the questioning on a particular area, one in which he is perhaps most competent, so you can expect each member to participate in the examination. Because time is limited, you may also expect some rather abrupt switches in the direction the questioning takes, so do not be upset by it. Normally, a board member will not pursue a single line of questioning unless he discovers a particular strength or weakness.

After each member has participated, the chairman will usually ask whether any member has any further questions, then will ask you if you have anything you wish to add. Unless you are expecting this question, it may floor you. Worse, it may start you off on an extended, extemporaneous speech. The board is not usually seeking more information. The question is principally to offer you a last opportunity to present further qualifications or to indicate that you have nothing to add. So, if you feel that a significant qualification or characteristic has been overlooked, it is proper to point it out in a sentence or so. Do not compliment the board on the thoroughness of their examination – they have been sketchy, and you know it. If you wish, merely say, "No thank you, I have nothing further to add." This is a point where you can "talk yourself out" of a good impression or fail to present an important bit of information. Remember, *you close the interview yourself.*

The chairman will then say, "That is all, Mr. _____, thank you." Do not be startled; the interview is over, and quicker than you think. Thank him, gather your belongings and take your leave. Save your sigh of relief for the other side of the door.

How to put your best foot forward

Throughout this entire process, you may feel that the board individually and collectively is trying to pierce your defenses, seek out your hidden weaknesses and embarrass and confuse you. Actually, this is not true. They are obliged to make an appraisal of your qualifications for the job you are seeking, and they want to see you in your best light. Remember, they must interview all candidates and a non-cooperative candidate may become a failure in spite of their best efforts to bring out his qualifications. Here are 15 suggestions that will help you:

1) Be natural – Keep your attitude confident, not cocky

If you are not confident that you can do the job, do not expect the board to be. Do not apologize for your weaknesses, try to bring out your strong points. The board is interested in a positive, not negative, presentation. Cockiness will antagonize any board member and make him wonder if you are covering up a weakness by a false show of strength.

2) Get comfortable, but don't lounge or sprawl

Sit erectly but not stiffly. A careless posture may lead the board to conclude that you are careless in other things, or at least that you are not impressed by the importance of the occasion. Either conclusion is natural, even if incorrect. Do not fuss with your clothing, a pencil or an ashtray. Your hands may occasionally be useful to emphasize a point; do not let them become a point of distraction.

3) Do not wisecrack or make small talk

This is a serious situation, and your attitude should show that you consider it as such. Further, the time of the board is limited – they do not want to waste it, and neither should you.

4) Do not exaggerate your experience or abilities

In the first place, from information in the application or other interviews and sources, the board may know more about you than you think. Secondly, you probably will not get away with it. An experienced board is rather adept at spotting such a situation, so do not take the chance.

5) If you know a board member, do not make a point of it, yet do not hide it

Certainly you are not fooling him, and probably not the other members of the board. Do not try to take advantage of your acquaintanceship – it will probably do you little good.

6) Do not dominate the interview

Let the board do that. They will give you the clues – do not assume that you have to do all the talking. Realize that the board has a number of questions to ask you, and do not try to take up all the interview time by showing off your extensive knowledge of the answer to the first one.

7) Be attentive

You only have 20 minutes or so, and you should keep your attention at its sharpest throughout. When a member is addressing a problem or question to you, give him your undivided attention. Address your reply principally to him, but do not exclude the other board members.

8) Do not interrupt
A board member may be stating a problem for you to analyze. He will ask you a question when the time comes. Let him state the problem, and wait for the question.

9) Make sure you understand the question
Do not try to answer until you are sure what the question is. If it is not clear, restate it in your own words or ask the board member to clarify it for you. However, do not haggle about minor elements.

10) Reply promptly but not hastily
A common entry on oral board rating sheets is "candidate responded readily," or "candidate hesitated in replies." Respond as promptly and quickly as you can, but do not jump to a hasty, ill-considered answer.

11) Do not be peremptory in your answers
A brief answer is proper – but do not fire your answer back. That is a losing game from your point of view. The board member can probably ask questions much faster than you can answer them.

12) Do not try to create the answer you think the board member wants
He is interested in what kind of mind you have and how it works – not in playing games. Furthermore, he can usually spot this practice and will actually grade you down on it.

13) Do not switch sides in your reply merely to agree with a board member
Frequently, a member will take a contrary position merely to draw you out and to see if you are willing and able to defend your point of view. Do not start a debate, yet do not surrender a good position. If a position is worth taking, it is worth defending.

14) Do not be afraid to admit an error in judgment if you are shown to be wrong
The board knows that you are forced to reply without any opportunity for careful consideration. Your answer may be demonstrably wrong. If so, admit it and get on with the interview.

15) Do not dwell at length on your present job
The opening question may relate to your present assignment. Answer the question but do not go into an extended discussion. You are being examined for a *new* job, not your present one. As a matter of fact, try to phrase ALL your answers in terms of the job for which you are being examined.

Basis of Rating
Probably you will forget most of these "do's" and "don'ts" when you walk into the oral interview room. Even remembering them all will not ensure you a passing grade. Perhaps you did not have the qualifications in the first place. But remembering them will help you to put your best foot forward, without treading on the toes of the board members.
Rumor and popular opinion to the contrary notwithstanding, an oral board wants you to make the best appearance possible. They know you are under pressure – but they also want to see how you respond to it as a guide to what your reaction would be under the pressures of the job you seek. They will be influenced by the degree of poise you display, the personal traits you show and the manner in which you respond.

EXAMINATION SECTION

SAFETY
EXAMINATION SECTION
TEST 1

DIRECTIONS: Each question or incomplete statement is followed by several suggested answers or completions. Select the one that BEST answers the question or completes the statement. *PRINT THE LETTER OF THE CORRECT ANSWER IN THE SPACE AT THE RIGHT.*

1. Which one of the following is an INCORRECT safety guideline?
    A. All working conditions and equipment should be considered carefully before beginning an operation.
    B. Aisles should be lighted properly.
    C. Personnel should be provided with protective clothing essential to safe performance of a task.
    D. In manual lifting, the worker must keep his knees straight and lift with the arm muscles.

1.___

2. Of the following, the supply item with the GREATEST susceptibility to spontaneous heating is
    A. alcohol, ethyl   B. kerosene
    C. candles   D. turpentine

2.___

Questions 3-7.

DIRECTIONS: Questions 3 through 7 are descriptions of accidents that occurred in a warehouse. For each accident, choose the letter in front of the safety measure that is MOST likely to prevent a repetition of the accident indicated.

SAFETY MEASURE

A. Posting warning signs
B. Redesign of layout or facilities
C. Repairing, improving or replacing supplies, tools or equipment
D. Training the staff in safe practices

3. After a new all-glass door was installed at the entrance to the warehouse, one of the employees banged his head into the door causing a large lump on his forehead when he failed to realize that the door was closed.

3.___

4. While tieing up a package with manila rope, an employee got several small rope splinters in his right hand and he had to have medical treatment to remove the splinters.

4.___

5. An employee discovered a small fire in a wastepaper basket but was unable to prevent it from spreading because all the nearby fire extinguishers were inaccessible due to skids of material being stacked in front of the extinguishers.

5.___

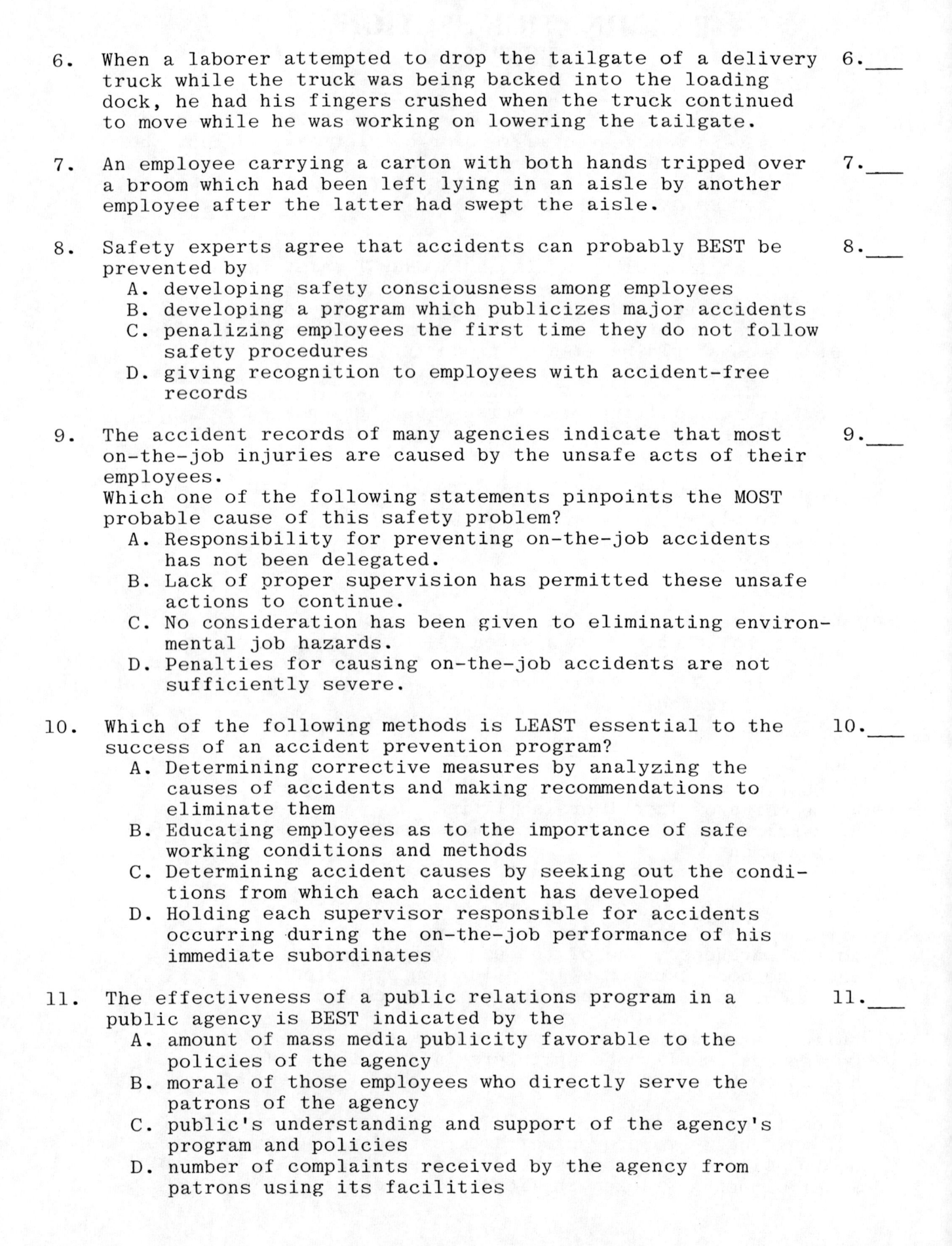

6. When a laborer attempted to drop the tailgate of a delivery truck while the truck was being backed into the loading dock, he had his fingers crushed when the truck continued to move while he was working on lowering the tailgate.

7. An employee carrying a carton with both hands tripped over a broom which had been left lying in an aisle by another employee after the latter had swept the aisle.

8. Safety experts agree that accidents can probably BEST be prevented by
   A. developing safety consciousness among employees
   B. developing a program which publicizes major accidents
   C. penalizing employees the first time they do not follow safety procedures
   D. giving recognition to employees with accident-free records

9. The accident records of many agencies indicate that most on-the-job injuries are caused by the unsafe acts of their employees.
   Which one of the following statements pinpoints the MOST probable cause of this safety problem?
   A. Responsibility for preventing on-the-job accidents has not been delegated.
   B. Lack of proper supervision has permitted these unsafe actions to continue.
   C. No consideration has been given to eliminating environmental job hazards.
   D. Penalties for causing on-the-job accidents are not sufficiently severe.

10. Which of the following methods is LEAST essential to the success of an accident prevention program?
    A. Determining corrective measures by analyzing the causes of accidents and making recommendations to eliminate them
    B. Educating employees as to the importance of safe working conditions and methods
    C. Determining accident causes by seeking out the conditions from which each accident has developed
    D. Holding each supervisor responsible for accidents occurring during the on-the-job performance of his immediate subordinates

11. The effectiveness of a public relations program in a public agency is BEST indicated by the
    A. amount of mass media publicity favorable to the policies of the agency
    B. morale of those employees who directly serve the patrons of the agency
    C. public's understanding and support of the agency's program and policies
    D. number of complaints received by the agency from patrons using its facilities

12. Buttered bread and coffee dropped on an office floor in a terminal are
    A. minor hazards which should cause no serious injury
    B. unattractive, but not dangerous
    C. the most dangerous types of office hazards
    D. hazards which should be corrected immediately

13. A laborer was sent upstairs to get a 20-pound sack of rock salt. While going downstairs and reading the printing on the sack, he fell, and the sack of rock salt fell and broke his toe.
    Which of the following is MOST likely to have been the MOST important cause of the accident?
    The
    A. stairs were beginning to become worn
    B. laborer was carrying too heavy a sack of rock salt
    C. rock salt was in a place that was too inaccessible
    D. laborer was not careful about the way he went down the stairs

14. A COMMONLY recommended safe distance between the foot of an extension ladder and the wall against which it is placed is
    A. 3 feet for ladders less than 18 feet in height
    B. between 3 feet and 6 feet for ladders less than 18 feet in length
    C. 1/8 the length of the extended ladder
    D. 1/4 the length of the extended ladder

15. The BEST type of fire extinguisher for electrical fires is the _____ extinguisher.
    A. dry chemical   B. foam
    C. carbon monoxide   D. baking soda-acid

16. A Class A extinguisher should be used for fires in
    A. potassium, magnesium, zinc, sodium
    B. electrical wiring
    C. oil, gasoline
    D. wood, paper, and textiles

17. The one of the following which is NOT a safe practice when lifting heavy objects is:
    A. Keep the back as nearly upright as possible
    B. If the object feels too heavy, keep lifting until you get help
    C. Spread the feet apart
    D. Use the arm and leg muscles

18. In a shop, it would be MOST necessary to provide a fitted cover on the metal container for
    A. old paint brushes   B. oily rags and waste
    C. sand   D. broken glass

19. Safety shoes usually have the unique feature of
    A. extra hard heels and soles to prevent nails from piercing the shoes
    B. special leather to prevent the piercing of the shoes by falling objects
    C. a metal guard over the toes which is built into the shoes
    D. a non-slip tread on the heels and soles

20. Of the following, the MOST important factor contributing to a helper's safety on the job is for him to
    A. work slowly   B. wear gloves
    C. be alert   D. know his job well

21. If it is necessary for you to lift one end of a piece of heavy equipment with a crowbar in order to allow a maintainer to work underneath it, the BEST of the following procedures to follow is to
    A. support the handle of the bar on a box
    B. insert temporary blocks to support the piece
    C. call the supervisor to help you
    D. wear heavy gloves

22. Of the following, the MOST important reason for not letting oily rags accumulate in an open storage bin is that they
    A. may start a fire by spontaneous combustion
    B. will drip oil onto other items in the bin
    C. may cause a foul odor
    D. will make the area messy

23. Of the following, the BEST method to employ in putting out a gasoline fire is to
    A. use a bucket of water
    B. smother it with rags
    C. use a carbon dioxide extinguisher
    D. use a carbon tetrachloride extinguisher

24. When opening an emergency exit door set in the sidewalk, the door should be raised slowly to avoid
    A. a sudden rush of air from the street
    B. making unnecessary noise
    C. damage to the sidewalk
    D. injuring pedestrians

25. The BEST reason to turn off lights when cleaning lampshades on electrical fixtures is to
    A. conserve energy
    B. avoid electrical shock
    C. prevent breakage of lightbulbs
    D. prevent unnecessary eye strain

KEY (CORRECT ANSWERS)

1. D
2. D
3. A
4. D
5. B

6. D
7. D
8. A
9. B
10. D

11. C
12. D
13. D
14. D
15. A

16. D
17. B
18. B
19. C
20. C

21. B
22. A
23. C
24. D
25. B

TEST 2

DIRECTIONS: Each question or incomplete statement is followed by several suggested answers or completions. Select the one that BEST answers the question or completes the statement. *PRINT THE LETTER OF THE CORRECT ANSWER IN THE SPACE AT THE RIGHT.*

1. The MOST important reason for roping off a work area in a terminal is to
   A. protect the public
   B. protect the repair crew
   C. prevent distraction of the crew by the public
   D. prevent delays to the public

   1.___

2. Shoes which have a sponge rubber sole should NOT be worn around a work area because such a sole
   A. will wear quickly
   B. is not waterproof
   C. does not keep the feet warm
   D. is easily punctured by steel objects

   2.___

3. When repair work is being done on an elevated structure, canvas spreads are suspended under the working area MAINLY to
   A. reduce noise   B. discourage crowds
   C. protect the structure D. protect pedestrians

   3.___

4. It is poor practice to hold a piece of wood in the hands or lap when tightening a screw in the wood.
   This is for the reason that
   A. sufficient leverage cannot be obtained
   B. the screwdriver may bend
   C. the wood will probably split
   D. personal injury is likely to result

   4.___

5. Steel helmets give workers the MOST protection from
   A. falling objects   B. eye injuries
   C. fire   D. electric shock

   5.___

6. It is POOR practice to wear goggles
   A. when chipping stone
   B. when using a grinder
   C. while climbing or descending ladders
   D. when handling molten metal

   6.___

7. When using a brace and bit to bore a hole completely through a partition, it is MOST important to
   A. lean heavily on the brace and bit
   B. maintain a steady turning speed all through the job
   C. have the body in a position that will not be easily thrown off balance
   D. reverse the direction of the bit at frequent intervals

   7.___

8. Gloves should be used when handling
   A. lanterns   B. wooden rules
   C. heavy ropes   D. all small tools

Questions 9-16.

DIRECTIONS: Questions 9 through 16, inclusive, are based on the ladder safety rules given below. Read these rules fully before answering these items.

LADDER SAFETY RULES

When a ladder is placed on a slightly uneven supporting surface, use a flat piece of board or small wedge to even up the ladder feet. To secure the proper angle for resting a ladder, it should be placed so that the distance from the base of the ladder to the supporting wall is 1/4 the length of the ladder. To avoid overloading a ladder, only one person should work on a ladder at a time. Do not place a ladder in front of a door. When the top rung of a ladder rests against a pole, the ladder should be lashed securely. Clear loose stones or debris from the ground around the base of a ladder before climbing. While on a ladder, do not attempt to lean so that any part of the body, except arms or hands, extends more than 12 inches beyond the side rail. Always face the ladder when ascending or descending. When carrying ladders through buildings, watch for ceiling globes and lighting fixtures. Avoid the use of rolling ladders as scaffold supports.

9. A small wedge is used to
   A. even up the feet of a ladder resting on an uneven surface
   B. lock the wheels of a roller ladder
   C. secure the proper resting angle for a ladder
   D. secure a ladder against a pole

10. An 8 foot ladder resting against a wall should be so inclined that the distance between the base of the ladder and the wall is _____ feet.
    A. 2   B. 5   C. 7   D. 9

11. A ladder should be lashed securely when
    A. it is placed in front of a door
    B. loose stones are on the ground near the base of the ladder
    C. the top rung rests against a pole
    D. two people are working from the same ladder

12. Rolling ladders
    A. should be used for scaffold supports
    B. should not be used for scaffold supports
    C. are useful on uneven ground
    D. should be used against a pole

13. When carrying a ladder through a building, it is necessary to
    A. have two men to carry it
    B. carry the ladder vertically
    C. watch for ceiling globes
    D. face the ladder while carrying it

14. It is POOR practice to
    A. lash a ladder securely at any time
    B. clear debris from the base of a ladder before climbing
    C. even up the feet of a ladder resting on slightly uneven ground
    D. place a ladder in front of a door

15. A person on a ladder should NOT extend his head beyond the side rail by more than _____ inches.
    A. 12   B. 9   C. 7   D. 5

16. The MOST important reason for permitting only one person to work on a ladder at a time is that
    A. both could not face the ladder at one time
    B. the ladder will be overloaded
    C. time would be lost going up and down the ladder
    D. they would obstruct each other

17. Many portable electric power tools, such as electric drills, have a third conductor in the power lead which is used to connect the case of the tool to a grounded part of the electric outlet.
    The reason for this extra conductor is to
    A. have a spare wire in case one power wire should break
    B. strengthen the power lead so it cannot easily be damaged
    C. prevent the user of the tool from being shocked
    D. enable the tool to be used for long periods of time without overheating

18. Protective goggles should NOT be worn when
    A. standing on a ladder drilling a steel beam
    B. descending a ladder after completing a job
    C. chipping concrete near a third rail
    D. sharpening a cold chisel on a grinding stone

19. When the foot of an extension ladder, placed against a high wall, rests on a sidewalk or another such similar surface, it is advisable to tie a rope between the bottom rung of the ladder and a point on the wall opposite this rung.
    This is done to prevent
    A. people from walking under the ladder
    B. another worker from removing the ladder
    C. the ladder from vibrating when ascending or descending
    D. the foot of the ladder from slipping

20. In construction work, practically all accidents can be blamed on the
    A. failure of an individual to give close attention to the job assigned to him
    B. use of improper tools
    C. lack of cooperation among the men in a gang
    D. fact that an incompetent man was placed in a key position

21. If it is necessary for you to do some work with your hands under a piece of heavy equipment while a fellow worker lifts up and holds one end of it by means of a pinch bar, one important precaution you should take is to
    A. wear gloves
    B. watch the bar to be ready if it slips
    C. insert a temporary block to support the piece
    D. work as fast as possible

22. Employees of the transit system whose work requires them to enter upon the tracks in the subway are cautioned not to wear loose fitting clothing.
    The MOST important reason for this caution is that loose fitting clothing may
    A. interfere when men are using heavy tools
    B. catch on some projection of a passing train
    C. tear more easily than snug fitting clothing
    D. give insufficient protection against subway dust

23. The MOST important reason for insisting on neatness in maintenance quarters is that it
    A. keeps the men busy in slack periods
    B. prevents tools from becoming rusty
    C. makes a good impression on visitors and officials
    D. decreases the chances of accidents to employees

24. Maintenance workers whose duties require them to do certain types of work generally work in pairs.
    The LEAST likely of the following possible reasons for this practice is that
    A. some of the work requires two men
    B. the men can help each other in case of accident
    C. there is too much equipment for one man to carry
    D. it protects against vandalism

25. A foreman reprimands a helper for actions in violation of the rules and regulations.
    The BEST reaction of the helper in this situation is to
    A. tell the foreman that he was careful and that he did not take any chances
    B. explain that he took this action to save time
    C. keep quiet and accept the criticism
    D. demand that the foreman show him the rule he violated

KEY (CORRECT ANSWERS)

1. A
2. D
3. D
4. D
5. A

6. C
7. C
8. C
9. A
10. A

11. C
12. B
13. C
14. D
15. A

16. B
17. C
18. B
19. D
20. A

21. C
22. B
23. D
24. D
25. C

EXAMINATION SECTION
TEST 1

DIRECTIONS: Each question or incomplete statement is followed by several suggested answers or completions. Select the one that BEST answers the question or completes the statement. *PRINT THE LETTER OF THE CORRECT ANSWER IN THE SPACE AT THE RIGHT.*

1. Of the following, the MOST important objective in accident analysis is to determine
    A. who is to blame
    B. how the accident could have been prevented
    C. whether the injured persons had received prescribed medical treatment
    D. the names of the persons involved and the exact nature of the injuries

2. Of the following statements, the one which would be of LEAST help in getting your men to do their work safely is to
    A. correct their unsafe work habits only if you think they may cause an accident
    B. see that they read and understand the safety rules they should follow
    C. talk to them often about the important of following safety regulations
    D. watch them at all times when they are working to see that they observe safety rules

3. The safety experts in your agency want to study accident reports as they are submitted in order to learn ways of preventing future accidents. You have been assigned to design a new accident report form which will help them achieve this goal.
Of the following, the item in the report that would be of MOST value to your safety experts for their purpose is
    A. the name and age of the accident victim
    B. a description of the working situation which led to the accident
    C. a statement from the foreman whether there was any carelessness involved
    D. a statement by the employee involved as to how the accident might have been prevented

4. A foreman should investigate every accident, including minor ones that do not involve injury, MAINLY because
    A. investigation of all accidents will help to increase the safety awareness of the employees
    B. each accident indicates a potential source of injury or damage
    C. the foreman will receive valuable experience in spotting hazardous conditions
    D. safety records should include all accidents regardless of seriousness

5. The following are methods used to prevent accidents. The one that is the MOST effective way to provide for safe and efficient operation of machines is to
   A. station guards on machines where physical hazards exist
   B. train employees in job procedures that will minimize accidents
   C. provide protective clothing and equipment for work on dangerous machines
   D. eliminate hazards by including safety considerations in the basic design

6. The MOST important element of preventive maintenance is
   A. calibration   B. lubrication
   C. inspection   D. cleaning

7. Of the following statements, the one that is MOST accurate is that a supervisor is
   A. not responsible for power tools used by his men
   B. not responsible for power tools used by his men if the men are properly trained in the use of these power tools
   C. always responsible for power tools used by his men
   D. responsible for power tools used by his men only if there has not been adequate time to train the men in the use of the power tools

8. Assume that your crew has been issued an item of safety equipment and the men refuse to wear it because it is not the brand they are used to.
   You, as supervisor, should
   A. let them work without it until you check with your superior
   B. stop the men from working and report the facts to your superior immediately
   C. warn them that they may lose compensation payments if there is an accident
   D. have the supply man issue the proper equipment

9. A steel measuring tape is undesirable for use around electrical equipment.
   The LEAST important reason is the
   A. magnetic effect
   B. short circuit hazard
   C. shock hazard
   D. danger of entanglement in rotating machines

10. When using a portable extension cord, the MOST important precaution to take is to
    A. see that the cord does not create a tripping hazard
    B. make sure that the cord does not touch any metal
    C. have a polarized plug at the end of the cord
    D. keep the cord clean and dry

11. Of the following, the one which is MOST likely to have the GREATEST effect in improving safety is
    A. holding foremen accountable for accidents of subordinates
    B. periodic safety inspections
    C. posting numerous safety bulletins
    D. providing each worker with periodic safety newsletters

12. The proper extinguisher to use on an electrical fire in an operating electric motor is
    A. sand
    B. water
    C. soda and acid
    D. carbon dioxide

13. When a container is used for flammable liquids, it usually presents the GREATEST hazard when it is
    A. empty but uncleaned
    B. empty and clean
    C. filled
    D. half-filled

14. Of the following cans, the SAFEST type of can to use for storing oil-soaked rags indoors is
    A. perforated sheet metal can with a sheet metal cover
    B. sheet metal can with a sheet metal cover
    C. sheet metal can without a cover
    D. sheet metal can with perforated sheet metal cover

15. To take the strain off the connections to an electrical plug, the knot which should be used is a(n)
    A. bowline
    B. hitch
    C. underwriter's
    D. square

16. In analyzing safety performance, the term *injury frequency rate* is used. This is defined as the number of disabling injuries per 1,000,000 man-hours worked.
    If an assistant supervisor has 80 men under him working 40 hours a week and 5 men suffered disabling injuries in a working period of 52 weeks, then the injury frequency rate would be closest to
    A. 25   B. 30   C. 35   D. 40

17. Of the following, the organization that MOST often certifies to the safety of individual pieces of equipment is the
    A. American Society for Testing Materials
    B. Underwriters' Laboratories, Inc.
    C. American Standards Association
    D. Association of Casualty and Surety Companies

18. The extinguishing agent in a soda-acid fire extinguisher is
    A. water
    B. carbon dioxide
    C. carbon tetrachloride
    D. calcium chloride solution

19. The proper technique for lifting heavy objects includes all of the following EXCEPT
    A. bending the knees
    B. placing the feet as far from the object as possible
    C. keeping the back straight
    D. lifting with the arms and legs

20. The one of the following methods which should NOT be used in treating portable wooden ladders is
    A. the application of a coat of clear lacquer
    B. thorough washing with soap and water
    C. the application of a coat of white paint
    D. the application of a coat of linseed oil

21. The MAIN reason for a requirement that defective material be removed from a job site as soon as possible is to
    A. prevent injuries
    B. reduce clutter in the area
    C. prevent accidental use of the material
    D. permit more efficient operation

22. The MAIN reason for reporting accidents is to
    A. prevent future accidents of the same type
    B. determine who was at fault
    C. prevent unwarranted lawsuits
    D. have a record of the causes of delays

23. Employees who must lift and carry stock items should be careful to avoid injury.
    When an employee lifts or carries stock items, which of the following is the LEAST safe practice?
    A. Keep the legs straight and lift with the back muscles
    B. Keep the load as close to the body as possible
    C. Get a good grip on the object to be carried
    D. First determine if the item can be lifted and carried safely

24. For warning and protection, the color *red* is usually for
    A. indicating high temperature stockroom areas
    B. floor markings
    C. location of first-aid supplies
    D. stop buttons, lights for barricades, and other dangerous locations

25. Reporting rattles, squeaks, or other noises in equipment to your maintenance supervisor is
    A. *bad*; too much attention to squeaks like these keep important safety problems from being noticed
    B. *bad*; each person should oil and care for his own equipment
    C. *good*; these sounds may mean that the equipment should be fixed
    D. *good*; it shows the supervisor that you are a good worker

KEY (CORRECT ANSWERS)

1. B
2. A
3. B
4. B
5. D

6. C
7. C
8. B
9. A
10. A

11. B
12. D
13. A
14. B
15. C

16. B
17. B
18. A
19. B
20. C

21. C
22. A
23. A
24. D
25. C

TEST 2

DIRECTIONS: Each question or incomplete statement is followed by several suggested answers or completions. Select the one that BEST answers the question or completes the statement. *PRINT THE LETTER OF THE CORRECT ANSWER IN THE SPACE AT THE RIGHT.*

1. An agency gives some of its maintenance employees instruction in first aid.
   The MOST likely reason for doing this is to
   A. eliminate the need for calling a doctor in case of accident
   B. reduce the number of accidents
   C. lower the cost of accidents to the agency
   D. provide temporary first aid

   1.___

2. If a fellow worker has stopped breathing after an electric shock, the BEST first-aid treatment is
   A. artificial respiration
   B. to massage his chest
   C. an application of cold compresses
   D. a hot drink

   2.___

3. If you had to telephone for an ambulance because of an accident, the MOST important information for you to give the person who answered the telephone would be the
   A. exact time of the accident
   B. place where the ambulance is needed
   C. cause of the accident
   D. names and addresses of those injured

   3.___

4. To use clean ice water as a treatment for burns is
   A. *good*, because it gives immediate relief from pain and seems to lessen the damaging effects of burns
   B. *bad*, because it has a tendency to cause frostbite which may develop into gangrene
   C. *good*, because ice water will destroy any bacteria at once
   D. *bad*, because the extremely cold temperature will cause a person to go into shock

   4.___

5. One of your men strained the muscles in his back when he attempted to lift a load that was extremely heavy.
   The treatment for this injury would include all of the following EXCEPT
   A. applying cold cloths or an ice bag to the back
   B. massaging the area
   C. resting the back in its most comfortable position
   D. rubbing the strained muscles with witch hazel

   5.___

6. A man who fainted in the terminal is now semiconscious. He is bleeding about the mouth and is in danger of choking on the blood.
He should be placed on his
   A. back, with his head slightly lower than his feet
   B. stomach, with his head turned to one side, lower than his feet
   C. back, with his feet slightly lower than his head
   D. stomach, with his head turned to one side, higher than his feet

7. When administering first aid to a helper suffering from shock as a result of falling off a high ladder, it is MOST important to
   A. cover the helper and keep him warm
   B. give the helper something to drink
   C. apply artificial respiration to the helper
   D. prop the helper up to a sitting position

8. If a co-worker's clothing gets caught in the gears of a machine in operation, the FIRST thing for a helper to do is to
   A. call the supervisor
   B. try to pull him out
   C. shut off the machine's power
   D. jam a metal tool between the gears of the machine

9. The one of the following which is the FIRST thing to do when a person gets an electric shock and is still in contact with the supply is to
   A. start artificial respiration immediately
   B. treat for burns
   C. cut the power if it takes no more than 5 minutes to locate the switch
   D. remove the victim from the contact by using a dry stick or dry rope

10. The one of the following that is the LEAST important health precaution for a worker to take is
    A. frequent washing
    B. shading his eyes from reflected light
    C. using an antiseptic on cuts
    D. wearing rubber gloves

11. Before entering a sewer which is known to contain dangerous gases, the able foreman will
    A. drop lighted matches down the manhole
    B. make sure all manholes in the vicinity are closed
    C. send one man down to determine the amount of gas present
    D. wait until the sewer has been ventilated

12. The one of the following that would MOST likely be the cause of a sewer explosion is
    A. a pressure relief valve installed in the main sewer line
    B. an unplugged opening left for a house connection
    C. naphtha discharged into the sewer by a cleaning establishment
    D. sewage of recent origin containing dissolved oxygen

13. In case of severe injury and where there is a possibility of broken bones, the MOST important precaution to take in giving first aid to an injured man is:
    A. Bundle him into an automobile and get him to a hospital as fast as possible
    B. Lower his feet and raise his head
    C. Move him no more than necessary and call a doctor
    D. Raise him to a sitting position and give him a drink of water

14. The logical reason that certain employees who work on the tracks carry small parts in fiber pails rather than steel pails is that fiber pails
    A. are stronger
    B. can't rust
    C. can't be dented by rough usage
    D. do not conduct electricity

15. While working on a certain track between stations, a helper notices a man standing on an adjacent track and suspects from the man's actions that he may have no business being there.
    The MOST reasonable procedure would be to
    A. continue working and ignore the man
    B. order the man to get off the tracks immediately
    C. ask the man what business he has being there
    D. hold the man for questioning by police

16. With respect to safety of personnel, it is probably LEAST important to
    A. have a place for each tool and put each tool in its place at the end of each day
    B. place each tool where it cannot fall down and hurt anyone when working on a job
    C. coat each tool with grease at the end of each day to prevent rust
    D. inspect carefully all tools to be used before beginning the day's work

17. Employees whose work requires them to enter upon the tracks are cautioned not to wear loose-fitting clothing. The MOST important reason for this caution is that loose-fitting clothing may
    A. interfere when they are using heavy tools
    B. catch on some projection of a passing train
    C. give insufficient protection against dust
    D. tear more easily than snug-fitting clothing

18. Recent safety reports indicate that a principal cause of injury to employees is *falls* while on a job. Such reports tend to emphasize that safety on the job is BEST assured by
    A. following every rule
    B. keeping alert
    C. never working alone
    D. working very slowly

19. The one of the following statements about a plug fuse that is MOST valid is that it should
    A. always be screwed in lightly to assure easy removal
    B. never be used to hold a coin in the fuse socket
    C. never be replaced by someone unfamiliar with the circuit
    D. always be replaced by a larger size if it burns out frequently

20. If a helper has frequent accidents, it is MOST likely that he is
    A. not physically strong enough to do the job
    B. simply one of those persons who is unlucky
    C. not paying enough attention to safe work habits
    D. trying too hard

21. A rule states that, *In walking on the track, walk opposite to the direction of traffic on that track if possible.*
    By logical reasoning, the PRINCIPAL safety idea behind this rule is that the man on the track
    A. is more likely to see an approaching train
    B. will be seen more readily by the motorman
    C. need not be as careful
    D. is better able to judge the speed of the train

22. The PRINCIPAL objection to using water from a hose to put out a fire involving live electrical equipment is that
    A. insulation may be damaged
    B. cast iron parts may rust
    C. serious electric shock may result
    D. a short-circuit will result

23. An electrician's knife should NOT be used to
    A. cut copper wires
    B. remove rubber insulation
    C. cut friction tape
    D. sharpen pencils

24. According to a safety report, a frequent cause of accidents to workers is the improper use of tools.
    The MOST helpful conclusion that you can draw from this statement is that
    A. most tools are difficult to use properly
    B. most tools are dangerous to use
    C. many accidents from tools are unavoidable
    D. many accidents from tools occur because of poor working habits

25. When a maintainer reports a minor trouble orally to his foreman, the MOST important information the foreman would require from the maintainer would be the
   A. type of trouble and its exact location
   B. names of all men with him when he discovered the trouble
   C. exact time the trouble was discovered
   D. work he was doing when he noted the trouble

KEY (CORRECT ANSWERS)

1. D
2. A
3. B
4. A
5. A

6. B
7. A
8. C
9. D
10. B

11. D
12. C
13. C
14. D
15. C

16. C
17. B
18. B
19. B
20. C

21. A
22. C
23. A
24. D
25. A

SAFETY
EXAMINATION SECTION
TEST 1

DIRECTIONS: Each question or incomplete statement is followed by several suggested answers or completions. Select the one that BEST answers the question or completes the statement. *PRINT THE LETTER OF THE CORRECT ANSWER IN THE SPACE AT THE RIGHT.*

1. The type of portable fire extinguisher which is *particularly* suited for extinguishing flammable liquid fires is the
    A. soda-acid type
    B. foam type
    C. pump tank type
    D. loaded stream type

2. The extinguishing agent in a soda-acid fire extinguisher is
    A. water
    B. hydrochloric acid
    C. sodium bicarbonate
    D. carbon dioxide

3. The MAIN reason for not permitting more than one person to work on a ladder at the same time is that
    A. the ladder might get overloaded
    B. several persons on the ladder might obstruct each other
    C. time would be lost going up and down the ladder
    D. several persons could not all face the ladder at one time

4. Safety on the job is BEST assured by
    A. keeping alert
    B. working only with new tools
    C. working very slowly
    D. avoiding the necessity for working overtime

5. A serious safety hazard occurs when a
    A. hardened steel hammer is used to strike a hardened steel surface
    B. soft iron hammer is used to strike a hardened steel surface
    C. hardened steel hammer is used to strike a soft iron surface
    D. soft iron hammer is used to strike a soft iron surface

6. Protective goggles should NOT be worn when
    A. standing on a ladder drilling a steel beam
    B. descending a ladder after completing a job
    C. chipping concrete near a third rail
    D. sharpening a cold chisel on a grinding stone

1.___

2.___

3.___

4.___

5.___

6.___

7. In an accident report, the information which may be MOST useful in DECREASING the recurrence of similar type accidents is the
   A. extent of injuries sustained
   B. time the accident happened
   C. number of people involved
   D. cause of the accident

8. A laborer was sent upstairs to get a 20-pound sack of rock salt. While going downstairs and reading the printing on the sack, he fell and the sack of rock salt fell and broke his toe.
   Which of the following is *most likely* to have been the most important cause of the accident? The
   A. stairs were beginning to become worn
   B. laborer was carrying too heavy a sack of rock salt
   C. rock salt was in a place that was too inaccessible
   D. laborer was not careful about the way he went down the stairs

9. Shoes which have a sponge rubber sole should NOT be worn around a work area because such a sole
   A. will wear quickly
   B. is not waterproof
   C. does not keep the feet warm
   D. is easily punctured by steel objects

10. Gloves should be used when handling
    A. lanterns
    B. wooden rules
    C. heavy ropes
    D. all small tools

11. Steel helmets give workers the MOST protection from
    A. falling objects
    B. eye injuries
    C. fire
    D. electric shock

12. It is POOR practice to wear goggles when
    A. chipping stone
    B. using a grinder
    C. climbing or descending ladders
    D. handling molten metal

13. In construction work, *almost all* accidents can be blamed on the
    A. failure of an individual to give close attention to the job assigned to him
    B. use of improper tools
    C. lack of cooperation among the men in a gang
    D. fact that an incompetent man was placed in a key position

14. If it is necessary for you to do some work with your hands under a piece of heavy equipment, while a fellow worker lifts up and holds one end of it by means of a pinch bar, one IMPORTANT precaution you should take is to
    A. wear gloves
    B. watch the bar to be ready if it slips
    C. insert a temporary block to support the piece
    D. work as fast as possible

15. The MOST important safety precaution to follow when using an electric drill press is to
    A. wear safety shoes
    B. drill at a slow speed
    C. use plenty of cutting oil
    D. clamp the work firmly

16. Assume that the top of a 12-foot portable straight ladder is placed against a wall but is not held by a man or fastened in any way. In order to be safe, the ladder should be placed so that the distance from the wall to the foot of the ladder is
    A. not over 3 feet
    B. not over 4 feet
    C. at least 4 feet
    D. at least 5 feet

17. A good safety rule to follow is that water should NOT be used to extinguish fires in or around electrical apparatus. Of the following, the PRIMARY reason for this is that water
    A. will damage the insulation
    B. will corrode the electrical conductors
    C. may cause the circuit fuse to blow
    D. may conduct electric current and cause a shock hazard

18. One should be extremely careful to keep open flames and sparks away from storage batteries when they are being charged because the
    A. sulphate given off during this operation is highly flammable
    B. hydrogen given off during this operation is highly flammable
    C. oxygen given off during this operation is extremely flammable
    D. static electricity of the battery may cause combustion

19. A good safety rule to follow is that an electric hand tool, such as a portable electric drill, should never be lifted or carried by its service cord. Of the following, the PRIMARY reason for this rule is that the
    A. tool might swing and be damaged by striking some hard object
    B. cord might be pulled off its terminals and become short circuited
    C. tool may slip out of the hand as it is hard to get a good grip on a slick rubber cord
    D. rubber covering of the cord might overstretch

20. When a man is working on a 15-foot ladder with its top placed against a wall, the MAXIMUM safe distance that he may reach out to one side of the ladder is
    A. as far out as he can reach lifting one foot off the rung for balance
    B. as far out as he can reach without bending his body more than 45° from the vertical
    C. one third the length of the ladder
    D. as far out as his arm's length

21. When NOT in use, oily waste rags should be stored in   21. __
    A. water-tight oak barrels
    B. open metal containers
    C. sealed cardboard boxes
    D. self-closing, metal containers

Questions 22-25.

DIRECTIONS: Each question consists of a statement. You are to indicate whether the statement is TRUE (T) or FALSE (F). *PRINT THE LETTER OF THE CORRECT ANSWER IN THE SPACE AT THE RIGHT.*

22. To help prevent accidents, gloves should be worn when   22. __
    handling rough wood or broken glass.

23. The safest and quickest way to remove a burnt-out light   23. __
    bulb from a ceiling fixture is to stand on a chair on top
    of a desk or table.

24. You should get help before lifting a large or heavy   24. __
    object which you believe is beyond your strength.

25. In lifting a heavy object, keep your feet together and   25. __
    never crouch down.

KEY (CORRECT ANSWERS)

1. B	11. A
2. A	12. C
3. A	13. A
4. A	14. C
5. A	15. D
6. B	16. A
7. D	17. D
8. D	18. B
9. D	19. B
10. C	20. D

21. D
22. T
23. F
24. T
25. F

TEST 2

DIRECTIONS: Each question or incomplete statement is followed by several suggested answers or completions. Select the one that BEST answers the question or completes the statement. *PRINT THE LETTER OF THE CORRECT ANSWER IN THE SPACE AT THE RIGHT.*

1. Safety on any job is BEST assured by
    A. working very slowly
    B. following every rule
    C. never working alone
    D. keeping alert

2. Of the following firefighting agents used in portable fire extinguishers, the one which is *most likely* to spread a flammable liquid fire is
    A. foam
    B. a solid stream of water
    C. carbon dioxide
    D. dry chemical

3. Transit employees are cautioned, as a safety measure, not to use water to extinguish fires involving electrical equipment. One logical reason for this caution is that the water
    A. will cause harmful steam
    B. will not extinguish a fire started by electricity
    C. may transmit electrical shock to the user
    D. may crack hot insulators

4. When carrying pipe, employees are cautioned against lifting with the fingers inserted in the ends. The *probable* reason for this caution is to avoid the possibility of
    A. dropping and damaging pipe
    B. getting dirt and perspiration on inside of pipe
    C. cutting the fingers on edge of pipe
    D. straining finger muscles

5. The MOST common cause for a workman to lose his balance and fall when working from an extension ladder is
    A. too much spring in the ladder
    B. sideways sliding of the top
    C. exerting a heavy pull on an object which gives suddenly
    D. working on something directly behind the ladder

6. Protective goggles SHOULD be worn when
    A. climbing a ladder
    B. reading a gage
    C. using a chipping hammer
    D. driving a hi-lo truck

7. An employee will *most likely* avoid accidental injury if he
   A. stops to rest frequently
   B. works alone
   C. keeps mentally alert
   D. works very slowly

8. Electrical helpers on the subway system are instructed in the use of fire extinguishers. The *probable* reason for including helpers in this instruction is that the helper
   A. cannot do the more important work
   B. may be the cause of a fire because of his inexperience
   C. may be alone when a fire starts
   D. will become interested in fire prevention

9. There are a few workers who are seemingly prone to accidents and who, regardless of their assigned job, have a higher accident rate than the average worker. If your co-worker is known to be such an individual, the BEST course for you to pursue would be to
   A. do most of the assigned work yourself
   B. refuse to work with this individual
   C. provide him with a copy of all rules and regulations
   D. personally check all safety precautions on each job

10. A rule of the transit system states that, "In walking on the track, walk opposite the direction of traffic on that track if possible." By logical reasoning, the *principal* safety idea behind this rule is that the man on the track
    A. is more likely to see an approaching train
    B. will be seen more readily by the motorman
    C. need not be as careful
    D. is better able to judge the speed of the train

11. Of the following types of fire extinguishers, the one that should NOT be used to extinguish a burning gasoline fire is
    A. soda acid   B. dry chemical
    C. carbon dioxide   D. liquified gas

12. It is NOT necessary to wear protective goggles when
    A. drilling rivet holes in a steel beam
    B. sharpening tools on a power grinder
    C. welding a steel plate to a pipe column
    D. laying up a cinder block partition

13. The MOST important reason for insisting on neatness in maintenance quarters is that it
    A. increases the available storage space
    B. makes for good employee morale
    C. prevents tools from becoming rusty
    D. decreases the chances of accidents to employees

14. There are many steel ladders and stairways installed in   14.___
    the subway for the use of transit workers. Their
    GREATEST danger is that they
    A. have sharp edges causing cuts
    B. are slippery when greasy and wet
    C. cause colds
    D. have no "give" and thus cause fatigue

15. Of the following, the MOST common result of accidents   15.___
    occurring while using hand tools is
    A. loss of limbs   B. loss of eyesight
    C. infection of wounds   D. loss of life

16. The one of the following extinguishing agents which should 16.___
    NOT be used on an oil fire is
    A. foam   B. sand
    C. water   D. carbon dioxide

17. The extinguishing agent in a portable soda-acid fire   17.___
    extinguisher is
    A. sodium bicarbonate   B. sulphuric acid
    C. carbon dioxide   D. water

18. A foam-type fire extinguisher extinguishes fires by   18.___
    A. cooling only   B. drenching only
    C. smothering only   D. cooling and smothering

19. The extinguishing agent in a soda-acid fire extinguisher   19.___
    is
    A. carbon dioxide
    B. water
    C. carbon tetrachloride
    D. calcium chloride solution

20. The proper extinguisher to use on an electrical fire in   20.___
    an operating electric motor is
    A. foam   B. carbon dioxide
    C. soda and acid   D. water

21. Transit workers are advised to report injuries caused by   21.___
    nails, no matter how slight.
    The MOST important reason for this rule is that this type
    of injury
    A. is caused by violating safety rules
    B. can only be caused by carelessness
    C. generally causes dangerous bleeding
    D. may result in a serious condition

Questions 22-25.

DIRECTIONS: Each question consists of a statement. You are to
              indicate whether the statement is TRUE (T) or FALSE (F).
              PRINT THE LETTER OF THE CORRECT ANSWER IN THE SPACE
              AT THE RIGHT.

22. The soda-and-acid type of extinguisher is effective for use on a flammable liquid fire.   22. ___

23. The carbon dioxide type of extinguisher is suitable for use on electrical fires.   23. ___

24. For good maintenance, the pressure cartridge in a cartridge-operated extinguisher should be replaced if the weight is ½ ounce less than is stamped on the cartridge.   24. ___

25. A paper fire is considered a Class A fire.   25. ___

KEY (CORRECT ANSWERS)

1. D
2. B
3. C
4. C
5. C

6. C
7. C
8. C
9. D
10. A

11. A
12. D
13. D
14. B
15. C

16. C
17. D
18. D
19. B
20. B

21. D
22. F
23. T
24. T
25. T

SAFETY
EXAMINATION SECTION
TEST 1

DIRECTIONS: Each question or incomplete statement is followed by several suggested answers or completions. Select the one that BEST answers the question or completes the statement. *PRINT THE LETTER OF THE CORRECT ANSWER IN THE SPACE AT THE RIGHT.*

1. There are two indicators used to determine the safety record of an agency. One is the "frequency of injury," and the other is the "severity of injury."
   The "frequency of injury" is considered a better indicator of the safety record because
   A. blind chance has a greater effect on "severity" than on "frequency"
   B. it is easier to record "frequency" than "severity"
   C. workers will pay more attention to "frequency" than to "severity"
   D. it is more difficult to determine the "severity" than the "frequency"

   1.___

2. It is frequently said that some people are "accident prone." This term should be applied ONLY to those people who
   A. fail to respond to safety training
   B. have accidents when the cause of the accident cannot be determined
   C. lack the physical capacity for their job
   D. do not have the skill required to do a certain job

   2.___

3. "Accidents frequently happen because a man 'daydreams' on the job." Of the following, the one that is CORRECT based on the previous sentence is:
   A. Accidents are most often caused by "daydreaming"
   B. The main cause of poor work is accidents
   C. A man who does not "daydream" is a good worker
   D. It is important for a man to pay attention to what he is doing

   3.___

4. Accidents can be classified as caused either by "unsafe acts" or "unsafe conditions." The one of the following that would be considered as "unsafe condition" is
   A. jumping over an obstruction on the floor
   B. poor lighting in a crowded cellar
   C. speeding in a motor vehicle
   D. use of the wrong tool for a job

   4.___

5. Of the following types of fires, a soda-acid fire extinguisher is NOT recommended for
   A. electric motor controls   B. waste paper
   C. waste rags   D. wood desks

   5.___

6. A foam-type fire extinguisher extinguishes fires by
    A. cooling only
    B. drenching only
    C. smothering only
    D. cooling and smothering

7. If an air-conditioning unit shorted out and caught fire, the BEST fire extinguisher to use would be a _____ extinguisher.
    A. water   B. foam
    C. carbon dioxide   D. soda acid

8. The one of the following diseases which may be caused by the pollution of drinking water by sewage is
    A. malaria   B. typhoid fever
    C. tuberculosis   D. muscular dystrophy

9. The type of portable fire extinguisher that is MOST effective in controlling a fire around live electrical equipment is the
    A. foam type   B. soda-acid type
    C. carbon-dioxide type D. water type

10. The hazards of electric shock resulting from operation of a portable electric tool in a damp location can be *reduced* by
    A. grounding the tool
    B. holding the tool with one hand
    C. running the tool at low speed
    D. using a baffle

11. The MAIN reason caretakers are advised to always wear protective goggles while changing a broken bulb is to avoid the danger of
    A. glare from the bulb
    B. pieces of glass getting in the eyes
    C. sparks from the bulb
    D. insects on or around the bulb socket

12. Of the following types of fire extinguishers, the one to use on an electrical fire is
    A. soda acid   B. carbon dioxide
    C. water pump tank   D. pyrene

13. The GREATEST number of injuries from equipment used in construction work result from
    A. carelessness of the operator
    B. poor maintenance of the equipment
    C. overloading of the equipment
    D. poor inspection of the equipment

14. Of the following, the BEST way a laborer can avoid accidents is to
    A. work slowly   B. be alert
    C. wear safety shoes   D. wear glasses

15. Of the following actions, the BEST one to take FIRST after smoke is seen coming from an electric control device is to
    A. shut off the power to it
    B. call the main office for advice
    C. look for a wiring diagram
    D. throw water on it

15.___

16. Of the following fire extinguishers, the one which should be provided for use in the elevator machine room is the
    A. carbon-dioxide type   B. soda-acid type
    C. foam type   D. loaded-stream type

16.___

17. Frequent deaths are reported as a result of running an automobile engine in a closed garage. Death results from
    A. suffocation
    B. carbon monoxide poisoning
    C. excessive humidity
    D. an excess of carbon dioxide in the air

17.___

18. As a veteran sewage treatment worker, you can BEST promote safety in your operations by
    A. carefully investigating and reporting the circumstances of any accident
    B. suggesting safer methods of operation
    C. training subordinates in proper safety
    D. disciplining subordinates who engage in unsafe acts

18.___

19. Oil soaked rags are BEST stored in a
    A. neat pile in a readily accessible corner
    B. metal container with a tight cover
    C. metal box that has holes for adequate ventilation
    D. closet on a shelf above the ground

19.___

20. The one of the following actions that is NOT the cause of injury when working with hand tools is
    A. working with defective tools
    B. using the wrong tool for the job
    C. working too carefully
    D. using a tool improperly

20.___

21. To safely lift a heavy object from the ground, you should keep your arms and elbows
    A. away from the body with your back bent
    B. away from the body with your back straight
    C. close to the body with your back bent
    D. close to the body with your back straight

21.___

Questions 22-25.

DIRECTIONS: Each question consists of a statement. You are to indicate whether the statement is TRUE (T) or FALSE (F). *PRINT THE LETTER OF THE CORRECT ANSWER IN THE SPACE AT THE RIGHT.*

22. The foam type extinguisher is not suitable for use on gasoline fires.   22.___

23. The first thing an employee should do when he sees a smoking electric wire is to throw water on the wire.   23.___

24. Many accidents are caused by carelessness of employees while at work.   24.___

25. If, at work, you are unable to lift a very heavy object, you should rest a couple of minutes and try again.   25.___

KEY (CORRECT ANSWERS)

1. A	11. B
2. A	12. B
3. D	13. A
4. B	14. B
5. A	15. A
6. D	16. A
7. C	17. B
8. B	18. C
9. C	19. B
10. A	20. C

21. D
22. F
23. F
24. T
25. F

TEST 2

DIRECTIONS: Each question or incomplete statement is followed by several suggested answers or completions. Select the one that BEST answers the question or completes the statement. *PRINT THE LETTER OF THE CORRECT ANSWER IN THE SPACE AT THE RIGHT.*

1. Assume that a fire breaks out in an electrical control panel board. Of the following types of portable fire extinguishers, the BEST one to use to put out this fire would be a
    A. dry-chemical type
    B. soda-acid type
    C. foam type
    D. water-stream type

    1.___

2. The MAJORITY of home accidents result from
    A. burns
    B. suffocation
    C. falls
    D. poisons

    2.___

3. A soda-acid fire extinguisher is recommended for use on fires consisting of
    A. wood or paper
    B. fuel oil or gasoline
    C. electrical causes or fuel oil
    D. paint or turpentine

    3.___

4. Of the following, the extinguishing agent that should be used on fires in flammable liquids is
    A. steam
    B. water
    C. foam
    D. soda and acid

    4.___

5. Of the following, the BEST way to put out a gasoline fire is to use
    A. a carbon dioxide extinguisher
    B. compressed air
    C. water
    D. rags to smother the blaze

    5.___

6. A heavy object should be lifted by first crouching and firmly grasping the object to be lifted. Then, the worker should lift
    A. using his back muscles and keeping his legs bent
    B. by straightening his legs and keeping his back as straight as possible
    C. using his arm muscles and keeping his back nearly horizontal
    D. using his arm muscles and keeping his feet close together

    6.___

7. The proper type of firefighting equipment to be used on an electrical fire is a
   A. soda-acid type extinguisher
   B. fire hose and water
   C. dry-chemical type extinguisher
   D. foam type extinguisher

8. While working on the job, you accidentally break a window pane. No one is around, and you are able to clean up the broken pieces of glass. It would then be BEST for you to
   A. leave a note near the window that a new glass has to be put in because it was accidentally broken
   B. forget about the whole thing because the window was not broken on purpose
   C. write a report to your supervisor telling him that you saw a broken window pane that has to be fixed
   D. tell your supervisor that you accidentally broke the window pane while working

9. The BEST way to remove some small pieces of broken glass from a floor is to
   A. use a brush and dust pan
   B. pick up the pieces carefully with your hands
   C. use a wet mop and a wringer
   D. sweep the pieces into the corner of the room

10. Employees should wipe up water spilled on floors immediately. The BEST reason for this is that water on a floor
    A. is a sign that employees are sloppy
    B. makes for a slippery condition that could cause an accident
    C. will eat into the wax protecting the floor
    D. is against health regulations

11. A carbon dioxide fire extinguisher is BEST suited for extinguishing
    A. paper fires   B. rag fires
    C. rubbish fires   D. grease fires

12. A pressurized water or soda-acid fire extinguisher is BEST suited for extinguishing
    A. wood fires   B. gasoline fires
    C. electrical fires D. magnesium fires

13. Assume that an officer, alone in a building at night, smells the strong odor of cooking or heating gas. In addition to airing the building and making sure that he is not overcome, it would be BEST for the officer to call
    A. his superior at his home and ask for instructions
    B. for a plumber from the department of public works
    C. 911 for police and fire help
    D. the emergency number at Con Edison

14. The one of the following which is the MOST common safety hazard in an office is
    A. a sharp pencil on a desk
    B. an open desk drawer
    C. lack of covers for electric computers
    D. lack of parallel alignment of desks

15. Which of the following situations is MOST likely to pose the greatest danger to safety?
    A. Buffing a main corridor to a high shine
    B. Leaving a door to a hall open at a 180° angle
    C. Opening the top two drawers of a four-drawer file cabinet
    D. Setting a desk at a 45° angle near a main aisle in an office

16. Safety experts agree that accidents can probably BEST be prevented by
    A. developing safety consciousness among employees
    B. developing a program which publicizes major accidents
    C. penalizing employees the first time they do not follow safety procedures
    D. giving recognition to employees with accident-free records

17. The accident records of many agencies indicate that most on-the-job injuries are caused by the unsafe acts of their employees. Which one of the following statements pinpoints the *most probable* cause of this safety problem?
    A. Responsibility for preventing on-the-job accidents has not been delegated.
    B. Lack of proper supervision has permitted these unsafe actions to continue.
    C. No consideration has been given to eliminating environmental job hazards.
    D. Penalties for causing on-the-job accidents are not sufficiently severe.

18. Which of the following methods is LEAST essential to the success of an accident prevention program?
    A. Determining corrective measures by analyzing the causes of accidents and making recommendations to eliminate them
    B. Educating employees as to the importance of safe working conditions and methods
    C. Determining accident causes by seeking out the conditions from which each accident has developed
    D. Holding each supervisor responsible for accidents occurring during the on-the-job performance of his immediate subordinates

19. Assume that you have a bad cold and take a strong decongestant pill before you come to work. You are scheduled, that day, to drive an official car to a supermarket to make an inspection. Of the following, it would be BEST for you to

A. drive to the store and make the inspection as usual
B. drive to the store very slowly and carefully, since you are not feeling well
C. explain to your supervisor that you should not drive that day
D. start out to make the inspection, but return to the office if you feel your driving ability is impaired

20. Of the following office supplies, the kind which you should usually be MOST careful to keep away from an open flame is
    A. carbon paper   B. ink
    C. paste   D. typing paper

21. The only one of the following types of fire extinguishers which should generally NOT be used to extinguish a gasoline fire is
    A. carbon dioxide   B. dry chemical
    C. foam   D. water

Questions 22-25.

DIRECTIONS: Each question consists of a statement. You are to indicate whether the statement is TRUE (T) or FALSE (F). *PRINT THE LETTER OF THE CORRECT ANSWER IN THE SPACE AT THE RIGHT.*

22. In directing the stream from a foam-type extinguisher at a fire, the extinguisher should be held upside down.

23. The carbon tetrachloride type of extinguisher is the most effective for use on electrical fires.

24. A soda-and-acid type of extinguisher should be refilled at least once in five years.

25. In lifting heavy articles, sanitation men should keep their feet wide apart.

KEY (CORRECT ANSWERS)

1. A	6. B	11. D	16. A	21. D
2. C	7. C	12. A	17. B	22. T
3. A	8. D	13. D	18. D	23. T
4. C	9. A	14. B	19. C	24. F
5. A	10. B	15. C	20. A	25. F

EXAMINATION SECTION

DIRECTIONS: Each question or incomplete statement is followed by several suggested answers or completions. Select the one that BEST answers the question or completes the statement. *PRINT THE LETTER OF THE CORRECT ANSWER IN THE SPACE AT THE RIGHT.*

1. The BEST indicator of reduced health hazard of a product is
    A. better sales
    B. fewer product defects
    C. fewer liability claims
    D. fewer returns
    E. government approval

    1.___

2. Workers exposed to toxic agents NOT known to cause cancer are *more likely* to have
    A. recurring complex examinations
    B. recurring simple examinations
    C. single, simple examinations
    D. single, complex examinations
    E. examinations each time exposures exceed TLV values

    2.___

3. An employer must FIRST make a written exposure determination when
    A. any employee may be exposed at the action level
    B. a regulated substance is released into the workplace air
    C. employee measurement indicates exposure at the action level
    D. employee measurement indicates exposure above the action level
    E. any substance is released into the air of the workplace

    3.___

4. Responsibilities of the industrial hygienic organization are to
    I. establish hygienic standards
    II. specify the design and quality of all types of personal protective equipment
    III. review work practices
    IV. make certain employees have been examined and approved for the job
    V. plan all operations to prevent unnecessary exposure

    The CORRECT answer is:
    A. I, IV, V
    B. II, V
    C. I, III, V
    D. I, II, III
    E. II, IV

    4.___

5. Program measurement of educational activities is *least likely* to involve
    A. consumers
    B. management
    C. workers
    D. supervisors
    E. members of the community

    5.___

6. The LEAST important consideration in measuring the effectiveness of programs to control occupational health hazards is
    A. labor turnover
    B. workers' compensation costs
    C. employee morale
    D. increased productivity
    E. sickness and employee absenteeism

7. Appendix B in the Federal Register includes
    I. physical and chemical data
    II. fire and explosion hazard data
    III. signs and symptoms
    IV. toxicology
    V. information on how to take air samples

    The CORRECT answer is:
    A. I, IV, V   B. I, II, IV   C. I, III, IV
    D. I, II, IV, V   E. I, II, V

8. ____ organizations are MOST involved in teaching and training programs.
    A. Supervisor   B. Medical
    C. Safety   D. Industrial hygiene
    E. Engineering

9. The PRIMARY benefit of an industrial hygiene program is
    A. good employee health
    B. control of occupational disease
    C. increased productivity
    D. increased employee efficiency
    E. accident prevention

10. Adequate summary records of concentrations of toxic substances like vinyl chloride monomer shall be maintained and held available for inspection for ____ year(s).
    A. 10   B. 5   C. 20   D. 30   E. 1

11. Which of the following is NOT a minimum requirement of the Standard Completion Program's employee training program?
    A. Review signs and symptoms of exposure to regulated materials
    B. Instructions to report any sign, symptom, or medical condition to the employer
    C. Training in the safe use of regulated substances
    D. Training of emergency procedure and protective equipment
    E. Training in the details of clean-up and disposal if spills occur

12. The BEST measure of conditions affecting comfort is(are)
    A. employee complaints   B. labor turnover
    C. employee morale   D. fewer product defects
    E. increased productivity

13. For maximum benefit, ____ is essential to any occupational health program.
    A. maintenance of accurate attendance records for personnel
    B. pre-employment psychological profiles of employees
    C. supervision of the health status of workers by qualified medical personnel
    D. screening programs which eliminate those workers who demonstrate susceptibility
    E. mandatory physical exams for all employees on a six-month basis

14. The employer must be informed of a potentially harmful work environment detected through examination of persons subjected to it because
    A. compensation policies require full disclosure
    B. administrative controls precede all others
    C. OSHA requires employers to keep accurate records
    D. employees are employer's biggest investment
    E. employer approval is necessary before the results can be supplied to the employee's personal physician

15. The objective of the Standards Completion Program is
    A. implementation of workroom level standards
    B. the expansion and completion of existing workroom level standards promulgated by the Department of Labor
    C. to help the employer to understand why and how to be in compliance with workroom level standards
    D. to develop standards to measure the performance of the industrial hygiene program
    E. the expansion and completion of uniform monitoring techniques of workroom level standards

16. As a result of manufactured products coming under a greater number of federal requirements, the industrial hygienist has increased liaison specifically with
    I. NRC   II. BRH   III. OSHA   D. CPSC   E. TOSCA

    The CORRECT answer is:
    A. I, II, V   B. I, III, V   C. I, II, III
    D. II, IV, V   E. I, II, IV

17. It is the employee's responsibility to
    A. develop and practice good habits of personal hygiene and housekeeping
    B. consult with safety professionals for aid in fulfilling his responsibilities
    C. conduct safety surveys at his work area
    D. maintain a work environment that assures maximum safety
    E. submit to a yearly physical exam

18. The ____ must consent to have the results of an occupational health program's physical exam supplied to the worker's personal physician or any other person or group.
    A. occupational physician   B. employee
    C. industrial hygienist   D. employer
    E. all of the above

19. When a personal monitoring discloses exposure to an employee beyond the OSHA standard, the individual should be notified in writing within ____ working days.
    A. 1-3   B. 20   C. 10   D. 5   E. 30

20. All of the following are reliable indications of improvement in environmental conditions affecting job efficiency EXCEPT
    A. increased productivity
    B. reduction in employee fatigue
    C. fewer product defects
    D. lower accident frequency rate
    E. lower labor turnover

21. Proper monitoring is NOT essential to the program measurement of
    A. environmental conditions affecting comfort
    B. health hazards of the firm's products
    C. air pollution control
    D. control of occupational health hazards
    E. environmental conditions affecting comfort

22. It is essential that outside help used for medical surveillance
    A. be familiar with conditions similar to those under which he is working
    B. have experience handling workers' compensation claims
    C. be familiar with OSHA requirements
    D. have access to available employee medical history information
    E. be familiar with the Standards Completion Program

23. Appendix C of the Federal Register is written for the
    A. employee   B. safety professional
    C. examining physician D. employer
    E. purchasing agent

24. All three types of medical surveillance activities proposed by the Standards Completion Program require
    A. examinations be made available to the employee
    B. preplacement medical exams
    C. worker completion of a health questionnaire
    D. medical surveillance procedures be made available if and when workers develop symptoms or have acute exposures
    E. all of the above

25. The engineering organization should notify the ____ organization whenever the introduction of new operations or processes is planned.
    I. supervisory   II. medical
    III. industrial hygiene   IV. safety
    V. purchasing

    The CORRECT answer is:
    A. I, III, IV   B. I, IV, V   C. III, IV
    D. I, V   E. II, III, IV

KEY (CORRECT ANSWERS)

1.	C	11.	E
2.	B	12.	A
3.	B	13.	C
4.	D	14.	C
5.	A	15.	B
6.	D	16.	D
7.	E	17.	A
8.	C	18.	B
9.	A	19.	C
10.	D	20.	E

21. B
22. C
23. C
24. D
25. E

EXAMINATION SECTION

DIRECTIONS: Each question or incomplete statement is followed by several suggested answers or completions. Select the one that BEST answers the question or completes the statement. *PRINT THE LETTER OF THE CORRECT ANSWER IN THE SPACE AT THE RIGHT.*

1. Employer compliance with OSHAct involves
    A. control of health exposures
    B. analysis of occupational safety and health statistics
    C. enforcement of employee obligations
    D. promulgating safety and health standards
    E. all of the above

2. What duties are triggered when the action level is reached?
    I. Exposure measurement   II. Engineering controls
    III. Medical surveillance   IV. Employee training
    V. Work practice controls

    The CORRECT answer is:
    A. I, II, III   B. I, III, IV
    C. I, IV, V   D. II, III, IV
    E. II, III, V

3. A serious penalty may be adjusted downward by as much as ____ percent.
    A. 40   B. 50   C. 25   D. 5   E. 10

4. The Federal Mine Safety and Health Amendment Act of 1977 transfers authority, for enforcement of mining safety and health, to the
    A. Department of the Interior
    B. Department of Labor
    C. Department of Health, Education and Welfare
    D. Bureau of Mines
    E. National Institute of Health

5. Safety and health regulations and standards which have the force and effect of law are issued by the
    A. Bureau of Labor Standards
    B. Occupational Safety and Health Administration
    C. Secretary of Health, Education and Welfare
    D. Secretary of Labor
    E. Assistant Secretary for Occupational Safety and Health

6. Court authority is necessary to enforce OSHAct to
    I. inspect when no advance notice has been given
    II. inspect records of industrial injuries and illnesses
    III. invoke criminal penalties
    IV. shut down an operation
    V. appeal OSHA actions

The CORRECT answer is:
A. I, II, III B. I, III, IV
C. II, III, IV D. III, IV
E. none of the above

7. A "serious violation" is defined as a condition
    A. where there is reasonable certainty that a hazard exists that can be expected to cause death or serious physical harm
    B. that has no direct or immediate relationship to job safety or health
    C. where there is a substantial probability that death or serious physical harm could result
    D. which is responsible for a fatality or multiple hospitalization incidents
    E. where a hazard is the result of unsafe work practices

8. The ____ is authorized by The Toxic Substance Control Act to require and obtain industry-developed data on the production, use and health effects of chemical substances and mixtures.
    A. Public Health Service Administration
    B. Occupational Safety and Health Administration
    C. National Center for Toxicological Research
    D. Environmental Protection Agency
    E. National Institute of Occupational Safety and Health

9. The Toxic Substances Control Act may LOWER the need for regulation by
    A. identifying hazards at the premarketing stage
    B. making OSHA more effective
    C. guarding against interagency duplication
    D. expanding research activities
    E. not issuing detailed workplace standards

10. How many other violations (exclusive of serious violations) that have a direct relationship to job safety and health and probably would not cause death or serious physical harm, must be found before any penalty can be imposed?
    A. 3   B. 1   C. 5   D. 10   E. 20

11. The ____ is(are) responsible for coordinating the technical aspects of the health program within the region.
    A. regional compliance officers
    B. area industrial hygienist
    C. area director
    D. national OSHA office
    E. regional office industrial hygienist

12. Horizontal Standards apply to
    A. establishing standards for engineering details
    B. all workplaces and relates to broad areas
    C. specific industries
    D. specific categories of workers
    E. establishing health and safety objectives

13. The ____ licenses and regulates the use of nuclear energy   13.___
    to protect public health and safety and the environment.
    A. Atomic Energy Commission
    B. National Institute for Occupational Safety and Health
    C. Radiological Assistance Program
    D. Bureau of Radiological Health
    E. Nuclear Regulatory Commission

14. Reviews of decisions of contested OSHA citations are con-   14.___
    ducted by the
    A. Occupational Safety and Health Review Commission
    B. U.S. Department of Labor
    C. Office of the Area Director
    D. State Supreme Court
    E. U.S. Court of Appeals

15. The compliance officer   15.___
    A. collects health hazard information
    B. shuts down operations where conditions of "imminent
       danger" exist
    C. collects appropriate samples
    D. investigates health complaints
    E. conducts an industrial hygiene inspection

16. OSHA defines "action level" as   16.___
    A. parity with the permissible exposure level
    B. concentrations below maximum allowable concentrations
    C. concentrations below minimum allowable concentrations
    D. one-half the permissible exposure level
    E. a reference point for control purposes

17. Which provision of the standard are employers obligated   17.___
    to when no employee is exposed to airborne concentrations
    of a substance in excess of the action level?
    A. Special training for employees
    B. Obtaining medical history statements
    C. Measuring employee exposure
    D. All of the above
    E. None of the above

18. Which of the following has the HIGHEST priority on OSHA's   18.___
    schedule of inspections?
    A. Response to employee complaints
    B. Random inspections of "high hazard industries"
    C. Response to community complaints
    D. Response to multiple hospitalizations incidents
    E. Response to reported conditions of "imminent danger"

19. A non-serious penalty has been adjusted from $1000.00 to   19.___
    $500.00. The LOWEST amount an employer may pay if the
    violation is corrected within the prescribed abatement
    period is
    A. $500   B. $375   C. $125   D. zero   E. $250

20. Chemicals that are exempt from premarket reporting are those
    I. produced in small quantities solely for research
    II. used for test marketing purposes
    III. determined not to present an unreasonable risk
    IV. intended for export only
    V. used exclusively for commercial purposes

    The CORRECT answer is:
    A. I, II, III   B. I, III, IV
    C. I, III, IV, V   D. II, III
    E. all of the above

21. The purpose of federal supervision of current state programs is to
    A. establish enforcement procedure
    B. determine excess exposures
    C. establish procedures for measuring exposure levels
    D. provide technical advice for sophisticated engineering systems
    E. achieve more uniform state inspection under federal standards

22. Which OSHA standard consists of TLVs?
    A. Performance   B. Health
    C. Design   D. Vertical
    E. Horizontal

23. How many federal working days of receipt of notice of the enforcement action does an employer have to contest an OSHA citation or penalty?
    A. 10   B. 15   C. 30   D. 45   E. 60

24. The PRINCIPAL federal agency engaged in research in the national effort to eliminate on-the-job hazards is the
    A. National Institute for Occupational Safety and Health
    B. Occupational Safety and Health Administration
    C. Environmental Protection Agency
    D. Food and Drug Administration
    E. Mine Safety and Health Administration

25. The area office updates the workplace inventory data
    A. semi-annually   B. yearly
    C. every 2 years   D. every 5 years
    E. following each inspection

KEY (CORRECT ANSWERS)

1. A	11. E	21. E
2. B	12. B	22. A
3. B	13. E	23. B
4. B	14. E	24. A
5. D	15. A	25. B
6. C	16. D	
7. C	17. C	
8. D	18. D	
9. A	19. E	

EXAMINATION SECTION

TEST 1

DIRECTIONS: Each question or incomplete statement is followed by several suggested answers or completions. Select the one that BEST answers the question or completes the statement. *PRINT THE LETTER OF THE CORRECT ANSWER IN THE SPACE AT THE RIGHT.*

1. An investigator uses *Forms A, B,* and *C* in filling out his investigation reports. He uses *Form B* five times as often as *Form A*, and he uses *Form C* three times as often as *Form B*.
   If the total number of all forms used by the investigator in a month equals 735, HOW MANY TIMES was *Form B* used?
   A. 150　　　B. 175　　　C. 205　　　D. 235

2. Of all the investigators in one agency, 25% work in a particular building. Of these, 12% have desks on the 14th floor.
   What PERCENTAGE of the investigators work in this building but do NOT have desks on the 14th floor?
   A. 12%　　　B. 13%　　　C. 22%　　　D. 23%

3. An investigator is given two reports to read. *Report P* is 160 pages long and takes the investigator 3 hours and 20 minutes to read.
   If *Report S* is 254 pages long and the investigator reads it at the same rate as he reads *Report P*, HOW LONG will it take him to read *Report S*? ___ hours ___ minutes.
   A. 4; 15　　　B. 4; 50　　　C. 5; 10　　　D. 5; 30

4. A team of 6 investigators was assigned to interview 234 people.
   If half the investigators conduct twice as many interviews as the other half, and the slow group interviews 12 persons a day, HOW MANY DAYS would it take to complete this assignment? ___ days.
   A. $4\frac{1}{4}$　　　B. 5　　　C. 6　　　D. $6\frac{1}{2}$

5. The investigators in one agency conduct an average of 12 interviews an hour from 10 A.M. to 12 noon and from 1 P.M. to 5 P.M. daily. The director of this agency knows from past experience that 20% of those called in to be interviewed are unable to keep the appointments that were scheduled.
   If the director wants his staff to be kept occupied with interviews for the entire time period that has been set aside for this function, HOW MANY appointments should be scheduled for each day?
   A. 86　　　B. 90　　　C. 96　　　D. 101

6. An investigator has a 430 page report to read. The first day, he is able to read 20 pages. The second day, he reads 10 pages more than the first day, and the third day, he reads 15 pages more than the second day.
If, on the following days, he continues to read at the same rate he was reading on the third day, he will COMPLETE the report on the ____ day.
   A. 7th   B. 8th   C. 10th   D. 11th

7. The 36 investigators in an agency are each required to submit 25 investigation reports a week. These reports are filled out on a certain form, and only one copy of the form is needed per report.
Allowing 20% for waste, HOW MANY packages of 45 forms a piece should be ordered for each weekly period?
   A. 15   B. 20   C. 25   D. 30

8. During the fiscal year, an investigative unit received $260 for stationery and telephone expenditures. It spent 43% for stationery and 1/3 of the balance for telephone service.
The amount of money that was left at the end of the fiscal year was MOST NEARLY
   A. $49   B. $50   C. $99   D. $109

Questions 9-10.

DIRECTIONS: Answer Questions 9 and 10 SOLELY on the data given below.

Number of days absent per worker (sickness)	1	2	3	4	5	6	7	8 or Over
Number of workers	96	45	16	3	1	0	1	0

Total Number of Workers: 500
Period Covered: Jan. 1, 2006 - Dec. 31, 2006

9. The TOTAL number of man days lost due to illness in 2006 was
   A. 137   B. 154   C. 162   D. 258

10. Of the 500 workers studied, the number who lost NO days due to sickness in 2006 was
    A. 230   B. 298   C. 338   D. 372

Questions 11-13.

DIRECTIONS: Answer Questions 11 to 13 SOLELY on the basis of the following paragraphs.

   The rise of urban-industrial society has complicated the social arrangements needed to regulate contacts between people. As a consequence, there has been an unprecedented increase in the volume of laws and regulations designed to control individual conduct and to govern the relationship of the individual to others. In a century, there has been an eight-fold increase in the crimes for which one may be prosecute

For these offenses, the courts have the ultimate responsibility for redressing wrongs and convicting the guilty. The body of legal precepts gives the impression of an abstract and evenhanded dispensation of justice. Actually, the personnel of the agencies applying these precepts are faced with the difficulties of fitting abstract principles to highly variable situations emerging from the dynamics of everyday life. It is inevitable that discrepancies should exist between precept and practice.

The legal institutions serve as a framework for the social order by their slowness to respond to the caprices of transitory fad. This valuable contribution exacts a price in terms of the inflexibility of legal institutions in responding to new circumstances. This possibility is promoted by the changes in values and norms of the dynamic larger culture of which the legal precepts are a part.

11. According to the above passage, the increase in the number of laws and regulations during the twentieth century can be attributed to the
    A. complexity of modern industrial society
    B. increased seriousness of offenses committed
    C. growth of individualism
    D. anonymity of urban living

12. According to the above passage, which of the following presents a problem to the staff of legal agencies? The
    A. need to eliminate the discrepancy between precept and practice
    B. necessity to apply abstract legal precepts to rapidly changing conditions
    C. responsibility for reducing the number of abstract legal principles
    D. responsibility for understanding offenses in terms of the real-life situations from which they emerge

13. According to the above passage, it can be concluded that legal institutions affect social institutions by
    A. preventing change
    B. keeping pace with its norms and values
    C. changing its norms and values
    D. providing stability

Questions 14-16.

DIRECTIONS: Answer Questions 14 through 16 SOLELY on the basis of information given in the passage below.

A personnel interviewer, selecting job applicants, may find that he reacts badly to some people even on first contact. This reaction cannot usually be explained by things that the interviewee has done or said. Most of us have had the experience of liking or disliking, of feeling comfortable or uncomfortable with people on first acquaintance, long before we have had a chance to make a conscious, rational decision about them. Often, too, our liking or disliking is transmitted to the other person by subtle processes such as gestures, posture, voice intonations, or choice of words. The point to be kept in mind is this:

the relations between people are complex and occur at several levels, from the conscious to the unconscious. This is true whether the relationship is brief or long, formal or informal.

Some of the major dynamics of personality which operate on the unconscious level are projection, sublimation, rationalization, and repression. Encountering these for the first time, one is apt to think of them as representing pathological states. In the extreme, they undoubtedly are, but they exist so universally that we must consider them also to be parts of normal personality.

Without necessarily subscribing to any of the numerous theories of personality, it is possible to describe personality in terms of certain important aspects or elements. We are all aware of ourselves as thinking organisms.

This aspect of personality, the conscious part, is important for understanding human behavior, but it is not enough. Many find it hard to accept the notion that each person also has an unconscious. The existence of the unconscious is no longer a matter of debate. It is not possible to estimate at all precisely what proportion of our total psychological life is conscious, what proportion unconscious. Everyone who has studied the problem, however, agrees that consciousness is the smaller part of personality. Most of what we are and do is a result of unconscious processes. To ignore this is to risk mistakes.

14. The passage above suggests that an interviewer can be MOST effective if he
    A. learns how to determine other peoples' unconscious motivations
    B. learns how to repress his own unconsciously motivated mannerisms and behavior
    C. can keep others from feeling that he either likes or dislikes them
    D. gains an understanding of how the unconscious operates in himself and in others

15. It may be inferred from the passage above that the *subtle processes such as gestures, posture, voice intonation, or choice of words* referred to in the first paragraph are USUALLY
    A. in the complete control of an expert investigator
    B. the determining factors in the friendships a person establishes
    C. controlled by a person's unconscious
    D. not capable of being consciously controlled

16. The passage above implies that various different personality theories are USUALLY
    A. so numerous and different as to be valueless to an investigator
    B. in basic agreement about the importance of the unconscious
    C. understood by the investigator who strives to be effective
    D. in agreement that personality factors such as projection and repression are pathological

Questions 17-19.

DIRECTIONS: Questions 17 through 19 are to be answered SOLELY on the basis of information contained in the following passage.

No matter how well the interrogator adjusts himself to the witness and how precisely he induces the witness to describe his observations, mistakes still can be made. The mistakes made by an experienced interrogator may be comparatively few, but as far as the witness is concerned, his path is full of pitfalls. Modern "witness psychology" has shown that even the most honest and trustworthy witnesses are apt to make grave mistakes in good faith. It is, therefore, necessary that the interrogator get an idea of the weak links in the testimony in order to check up on them in the event that something appears to be strange or not quite satisfactory.

Unfortunately, modern witness psychology does not yet offer any means of directly testing the credibility of testimony. It lacks precision and method, in spite of worthwhile attempts on the part of learned men. At the same time, witness psychology, through the gathering of many experiences concerning the weaknesses of human testimony, has been of invaluable service. It shows clearly that only evidence of a technical nature has absolute value as proof.

Testimony may be separated into the following stages: (1) perception; (2) observation; (3) mind fixation of the observed occurrences, in which fantasy, association of ideas, and personal judgment participate; (4) expression in oral or written form, where the testimony is transferred from one witness to another or to the interrogator.

Each of these stages offers innumerable possibilities for the distortion of testimony.

17. The passage above indicates that having witnesses talk to each other before testifying is a practice which is GENERALLY
    A. *desirable*, since the witnesses will be able to correct each other's errors in observation before testimony
    B. *undesirable*, since the witnesses will collaborate on one story to tell the investigator
    C. *undesirable*, since one witness may distort his testimony because of what another witness may erroneously say
    D. *desirable*, since witnesses will become aware of discrepancies in their own testimony and can point out the discrepancies to the investigator

18. According to the above passage, the one of the following which would be the MOST reliable for use as evidence would be the testimony of a
    A. handwriting expert about a signature on a forged check
    B. trained police officer about the identity of a criminal
    C. laboratory technician about an accident he has observed
    D. psychologist who has interviewed any witnesses who relate conflicting stories

19. Concerning the validity of evidence, it is CLEAR from the above passage that
    A. only evidence of a technical nature is at all valuable
    B. the testimony of witnesses is so flawed that it is usually valueless
    C. an investigator, by knowing modern witness psychology, will usually be able to perceive mistaken testimony
    D. an investigator ought to expect mistakes in even the most reliable witness testimony

Questions 20-21.

DIRECTIONS: Answer Questions 20 and 21 SOLELY on the basis of information given in the passage below.

Since we generally assure informants that what they say is confidential, we are not free to tell one informant what the other has told us. Even if the informant says, "I don't care who knows it; tell anybody you want to," we find it wise to treat the interview as confidential. An interviewer who relates to some informants what other informants have told him is likely to stir up anxiety and suspicion. Of course, the interviewer may be able to tell an informant what he has heard without revealing the source of his information. This may be perfectly appropriate where a story has wide currency so that an informant cannot infer the source of the information. But if an event is not widely known, the mere mention of it may reveal to one informant what another informant has said about the situation. How can the data be cross-checked in these circumstances?

20. The passage above IMPLIES that the anxiety and suspicion an interviewer may arouse by telling what has been learned in other interviews is due to the
    A. lack of trust the person interviewed may have in the interviewer's honesty
    B. troublesome nature of the material which the interviewer has learned in other interviews
    C. fact that the person interviewed may not believe that permission was given to repeat the information
    D. fear of the person interviewed that what he is telling the interviewer will be repeated

21. The paragraph above is MOST likely part of a longer passage dealing with
    A. ways to verify data gathered in interviews
    B. the various anxieties a person being interviewed may feel
    C. the notion that people sometimes say things they do not mean
    D. ways an interviewer can avoid seeming suspicious

Questions 22-23.

DIRECTIONS: Answer Questions 22 and 23 SOLELY on the basis of information given below.

The ability to interview rests not on any single trait, but on a vast complex of them. Habits, skills, techniques, and attitudes are all involved. Competence in interviewing is acquired only after careful and diligent study, prolonged practice (preferably under supervision), and a good bit of trial and error; for interviewing is not an exact science, it is an art. Like many other arts, however, it can and must draw on science in several of its aspects.

There is always a place for individual initiative, for imaginative innovations, and for new combinations of old approaches. The skilled interviewer cannot be bound by a set of rules. Likewise, there is not a set of rules which can guarantee to the novice that his interviewing will be successful. There are, however, some accepted, general guideposts which may help the beginner to avoid mistakes, learn how to conserve his efforts, and establish effective working relationships with interviewees; to accomplish, in short, what he sets out to do.

22. According to the passage above, rules and standard techniques for interviewing are
    A. helpful for the beginner, but useless for the experienced, innovative interviewer
    B. destructive of the innovation and initiative needed for a good interviewer
    C. useful for even the experienced interviewer, who may, however, sometimes go beyond them
    D. the means by which nearly anybody can become an effective interviewer

23. According to the passage above, the one of the following which is a PREREQUISITE to competent interviewing is
    A. avoid mistakes   B. study and practice
    C. imaginative innovation   D. natural aptitude

Questions 24-27.

DIRECTIONS: Answer Questions 24 through 27 SOLELY on the basis of information given in the following paragraph.

The question of what material is relevant is not as simple as it might seem. Frequently, material which seems irrelevant to the inexperienced has, because of the common tendency to disguise and distort and misplace one's feelings, considerable significance. It may be necessary to let the client "ramble on" for a while in order to clear the decks, as it were, so that he may get down to things that really are on his mind. On the other hand, with an already disturbed person, it may be important for the interviewer to know when to discourage further elaboration of upsetting material. This is especially the case where the worker would be unable to do anything about it. An inexperienced interviewer might, for instance, be intrigued with the bizarre elaboration of material that the psychotic produces, but further elaboration of this might encourage the client in his instability. A too random discussion may indicate that the interviewee is not certain in what areas the interviewer is prepared to help him, and he may be seeking some direction. Or again, satisfying though it may be for the interviewer to have the interviewee tell him intimate details, such revelations sometimes need to be checked or encouraged only in small doses. An interviewee who has "talked too much" often reveals subsequent anxiety. This is illustrated by the fact that frequently after a "confessional" interview, the interviewee surprises the interviewer by being withdrawn, inarticulate, or hostile, or by breaking the next appointment.

24. Sometimes a client may reveal certain personal information to an interviewer and subsequently may feel anxious about this revelation.
    If, during an interview, a client begins to discuss very personal matters, it would be BEST to
    A. tell the client, in no uncertain terms, that you're not interested in personal details
    B. ignore the client at this point
    C. encourage the client to elaborate further on the details
    D. inform the client that the information seems to be very personal

25. The author indicates that clients with severe psychological disturbances pose an especially difficult problem for the inexperienced interviewer.
    The DIFFICULTY lies in the possibility of the client
    A. becoming physically violent and harming the interviewer
    B. *rambling on* for a while
    C. revealing irrelevant details which may be followed by cancelled appointments
    D. reverting to an unstable state as a result of interview material

26. An interviewer should be constantly alert to the possibility of obtaining clues from the client as to the problem areas.
    According to the above passage, a client who discusses topics at random may be
    A. unsure of what problems the interviewer can provide help with
    B. reluctant to discuss intimate details
    C. trying to impress the interviewer with his knowledge
    D. deciding what relevant material to elaborate on

27. The evaluation of a client's responses may reveal substantial information that may aid the interviewer in assessing the problem areas that are of concern to the client.
    Responses that seemed irrelevant at the time of the interview may be of significance because
    A. considerable significance is attached to all irrelevant material
    B. emotional feelings are frequently masked
    C. an initial *rambling on* is often a prelude to what is actually bothering the client
    D. disturbed clients often reveal subsequent anxiety

Questions 28-30.

DIRECTIONS: Answer Questions 28 through 30 SOLELY on the basis of the following paragraph.

The physical setting of the interview may determine its entire potentiality. Some degree of privacy and a comfortable relaxed atmosphere are important. The interviewee is not encouraged to give much more than his name and address if the interviewer seems busy with other things, if people are rushing about, if there are distracting noises. He has a right to feel that, whether the interview lasts five minutes or an hour, he has, for that time, the undivided attention of the interviewer. Interruptions, telephone calls, and so on, should be reduced to a minimum. If the interviewee has waited in a crowded room for what seems to him an interminably long period, he is naturally in no mood to sit down and discuss what is on his mind. Indeed, by that time, the primary thing on his mind may be his irritation at being kept waiting, and he frequently feels it would be impolite to express this. If a wait or interruptions have been unavoidable, it is always helpful to give the client some recognition that these are disturbing and that we can naturally understand that they make it more difficult for him to proceed. At the same time, if he protests that they have not troubled him, the interviewer can best accept his statements at their face value, as further insistence that they must have been disturbing may be interpreted by him as accusing, and he may conclude that the interviewer has been personally hurt by his irritation.

28. Distraction during an interview may tend to limit the client's responses.
    In a case where an interruption has occurred, it would be BEST for the investigator to
    A. terminate this interview and have it rescheduled for another time period
    B. ignore the interruption since it is not continuous
    C. express his understanding that the distraction can cause the client to feel disturbed
    D. accept the client's protests that he has been troubled by the interruption

29. To maximize the rapport that can be established with the client, an appropriate physical setting is necessary. At the very least, some privacy would be necessary.
    In ADDITION, the interviewer should
    A. always appear to be busy in order to impress the client
    B. focus his attention only on the client
    C. accept all the client's statements as being valid
    D. stress the importance of the interview to the client

30. Clients who have been waiting quite some time for their interview may, justifiably, become upset.
    However, a client may initially attempt to mask these feelings because he may
    A. personally hurt the interviewer
    B. want to be civil
    C. feel that the wait was unavoidable
    D. fear the consequences of his statement

KEY (CORRECT ANSWERS)

1.	B	11.	A	21.	A
2.	C	12.	B	22.	C
3.	D	13.	D	23.	B
4.	D	14.	D	24.	D
5.	B	15.	C	25.	D
6.	D	16.	B	26.	A
7.	C	17.	C	27.	B
8.	C	18.	A	28.	C
9.	D	19.	D	29.	B
10.	C	20.	D	30.	B

TEST 2

DIRECTIONS: Each question or incomplete statement is followed by several suggested answers or completions. Select the one that BEST answers the question or completes the statement. *PRINT THE LETTER OF THE CORRECT ANSWER IN THE SPACE AT THE RIGHT.*

Questions 1-5.

DIRECTIONS: In Questions 1 through 5, choose the sentence which is BEST from the point of view of English usage suitable for a business report.

1. A. The client's receiving of public assistance checks at two different addresses were disclosed by the investigation.
   B. The investigation disclosed that the client was receiving public assistance checks at two different addresses.
   C. The client was found out by the investigation to be receiving public assistance checks at two different addresses.
   D. The client has been receiving public assistance checks at two different addresses, disclosed the investigation.

   1.___

2. A. The investigation of complaints are usually handled by this unit, which deals with internal security problems in the department.
   B. This unit deals with internal security problems in the department; usually investigating complaints.
   C. Investigating complaints is this unit's job, being that it handles internal security problems in the department.
   D. This unit deals with internal security problems in the department and usually investigates complaints.

   2.___

3. A. The delay in completing this investigation was caused by difficulty in obtaining the required documents from the candidate.
   B. Because of difficulty in obtaining the required documents from the candidate is the reason that there was a delay in completing this investigation.
   C. Having had difficulty in obtaining the required documents from the candidate, there was a delay in completing this investigation.
   D. Difficulty in obtaining the required documents from the candidate had the affect of delaying the completion of this investigation.

   3.___

4. A. This report, together with documents supporting our recommendation, are being submitted for your approval.
   B. Documents supporting our recommendation is being submitted with the report for your approval.

   4.___

C. This report, together with documents supporting our recommendation, is being submitted for your approval.
D. The report and documents supporting our recommendation is being submitted for your approval.

5. A. Several people were interviewed and numerous letters were sent before this case was completed.
B. Completing this case, interviewing several people and sending numerous letters were necessary.
C. To complete this case needed interviewing several people and sending numerous letters.
D. Interviewing several people and sending numerous letters was necessary to complete the case.

Questions 6-20.

DIRECTIONS: For each of the sentences numbered 6 to 20, select from the options given below the MOST applicable choice, and mark your answer accordingly.

A. The sentence is correct.
B. The sentence contains a spelling error only.
C. The sentence contains an English grammar error only.
D. The sentence contains both a spelling error and an English grammar error.

6. He is a very dependible person whom we expect will be an asset to this division.

7. An investigator often finds it necessary to be very diplomatic when conducting an interview.

8. Accurate detail is especially important if court action results from an investigation.

9. The report was signed by him and I since we conducted the investigation jointly.

10. Upon receipt of the complaint, an inquiry was begun.

11. An employee has to organize his time so that he can handle his workload efficiently.

12. It was not apparant that anyone was living at the address given by the client.

13. According to regulations, there is to be at least three attempts made to locate the client.

14. Neither the inmate nor the correction officer was willing to sign a formal statement.

15. It is our opinion that one of the persons interviewed were lying.

16. We interviewed both clients and departmental personel in   16.____
    the course of this investigation.

17. It is concievable that further research might produce   17.____
    additional evidence.

18. There are too many occurences of this nature to ignore.   18.____

19. We cannot accede to the candidate's request.   19.____

20. The submission of overdue reports is the reason that   20.____
    there was a delay in completion of this investigation.

Questions 21-25.

DIRECTIONS: Each of Questions 21 to 25 consists of three sentences
              lettered A, B, and C. In each of these questions, one
              of the sentences may contain an error in grammar, sen-
              tence structure, or punctuation, or all three sentences
              may be correct. If one of the sentences in a question
              contains an error in grammar, sentence structure, or
              punctuation, print in the space on the right the capital
              letter preceding the sentence which contains the error.
              If all three sentences are correct, print the letter D.

21. A. Mr. Smith appears to be less competent than I in   21.____
       performing these duties.
    B. The supervisor spoke to the employee, who had made
       the error, but did not reprimand him.
    C. When he found the book lying on the table, he immedi-
       ately notified the owner.

22. A. Being locked in the desk, we were certain that the   22.____
       papers would not be taken.
    B. It wasn't I who dictated the telegram; I believe it
       was Eleanor.
    C. You should interview whoever comes to the office today.

23. A. The clerk was instructed to set the machine on the   23.____
       table before summoning the manager.
    B. He said that he was not familiar with those kind of
       activities.
    C. A box of pencils, in addition to erasers and blotters,
       was included in the shipment of supplies.

24. A. The supervisor remarked, "Assigning an employee to   24.____
       the proper type of work is not always easy."
    B. The employer found that each of the applicants were
       qualified to perform the duties of the position.
    C. Any competent student is permitted to take this course
       if he obtains the consent of the instructor.

25. A. The prize was awarded to the employee whom the judges believed to be most deserving.   25. ___
    B. Since the instructor believes this book is the better of the two, he is recommending it for use in the school.
    C. It was obvious to the employees that the completion of the task by the scheduled date would require their working overtime.

KEY (CORRECT ANSWERS)

1. B
2. D
3. A
4. C
5. A

6. D
7. A
8. A
9. C
10. A

11. B
12. B
13. C
14. A
15. C

16. B
17. B
18. B
19. A
20. C

21. B
22. A
23. B
24. B
25. D

PREPARING WRITTEN MATERIAL
EXAMINATION SECTION
TEST 1

DIRECTIONS: Each question or incomplete statement is followed by several suggested answers or completions. Select the one that BEST answers the question or completes the statement. *PRINT THE LETTER OF THE CORRECT ANSWER IN THE SPACE AT THE RIGHT.*

Questions 1-4.

DIRECTIONS: Questions 1 through 4 each consist of a sentence which may or may not be an example of good English. The underlined parts of each sentence may be correct or incorrect. Examine each sentence, considering grammar, punctuation, spelling, and capitalization. If the English usage in the underlined parts of the sentence given is better than any of the changes in the underlined words suggested in options B, C, or D, choose option A. If the changes in the underlined words suggested in options B, C, or D would make the sentence correct, choose the correct option. Do not choose an option that will change the meaning of the sentence.

1. This <u>Fall</u>, the office will be closed on <u>Columbus Day, October</u> 9th.
   A. Correct as is
   B. fall...Columbus Day, October
   C. Fall...columbus day, October
   D. fall...Columbus Day, october
1.___

2. There <u>weren't no</u> paper in the supply closet.
   A. Correct as is   B. weren't any
   C. wasn't any   D. wasn't no
2.___

3. The <u>alphabet, or A to Z sequence are</u> the basis of most filing systems.
   A. Correct as is
   B. alphabet, or A to Z sequence, is
   C. alphabet, or A to Z sequence, are
   D. alphabet, or A too Z sequence, is
3.___

4. The Office Aide checked the <u>register and finding</u> the date of the meeting.
   A. Correct as is   B. regaster and finding
   C. register and found   D. regaster and found
4.___

Questions 5-10.

DIRECTIONS: Questions 5 through 10 consist of sentences which contain examples of correct or incorrect English usage. Examine each sentence with reference to grammar, spelling, punctuation, and capitalization. Choose one of the following options that would be BEST for correct English usage:
    A. The sentence is correct
    B. There is one mistake
    C. There are two mistakes
    D. There are three mistakes

5. Mrs. Fitzgerald came to the 59th Precinct to retreive her property which were stolen earlier in the week.

6. The two officer's responded to the call, only to find that the perpatrator and the victim have left the scene.

7. Mr. Coleman called the 61st Precinct to report that, upon arriving at his store, he discovered that there was a large hole in the wall and that three boxes of radios were missing.

8. The Administrative Lieutenant of the 62nd Precinct held a meeting which was attended by all the civilians, assigned to the Precinct.

9. Three days after the robbery occured the detective apprahended two suspects and recovered the stolen items.

10. The Community Affairs Officer of the 64th Precinct is the liaison between the Precinct and the community; he works closely with various community organizations, and elected officials.

Questions 11-18.

DIRECTIONS: Questions 11 through 18 are to be answered on the basis of the following paragraph, which contains some deliberate errors in spelling and/or grammar and/or punctuation. Each line of the paragraph is preceded by a number. There are 9 lines and 9 numbers.

Line No.	Paragraph Line
1	The protection of life and proporty are, one of
2	the oldest and most important functions of a city.
3	New York city has it's own full-time police Agency.
4	The police Department has the power an it shall
5	be there duty to preserve the Public piece,
6	prevent crime detect and arrest offenders, supress
7	riots, protect the rites of persons and property, etc.
8	The maintainance of sound relations with the community they
9	serve is an important function of law enforcement officers

11. How many errors are contained in line one? 11.___
     A. One   B. Two   C. Three   D. None

12. How many errors are contained in line two? 12.___
     A. One   B. Two   C. Three   D. None

13. How many errors are contained in line three? 13.___
     A. One   B. Two   C. Three   D. None

14. How many errors are contained in line four? 14.___
     A. One   B. Two   C. Three   D. None

15. How many errors are contained in line five? 15.___
     A. One   B. Two   C. Three   D. None

16. How many errors are contained in line six? 16.___
     A. One   B. Two   C. Three   D. None

17. How many errors are contained in line seven? 17.___
     A. One   B. Two   C. Three   D. None

18. How many errors are contained in line eight? 18.___
     A. One   B. Two   C. Three   D. None

19. In the sentence, *The candidate wants to file his application for preference before it is too late*, the word *before* is used as a(n) 19.___
     A. preposition   B. subordinating conjunction
     C. pronoun   D. adverb

20. The one of the following sentences which is grammatically PREFERABLE to the others is: 20.___
     A. Our engineers will go over your blueprints so that you may have no problems in construction.
     B. For a long time he had been arguing that we, not he, are to blame for the confusion.
     C. I worked on this automobile for two hours and still cannot find out what is wrong with it.
     D. Accustomed to all kinds of hardships, fatigue seldom bothers veteran policemen.

KEY (CORRECT ANSWERS)

1. A		11. C
2. C		12. D
3. B		13. C
4. C		14. B
5. C		15. C
6. D		16. B
7. A		17. A
8. C		18. A
9. C		19. B
10. B		20. A

TEST 2

DIRECTIONS: Each question or incomplete statement is followed by several suggested answers or completions. Select the one that BEST answers the question or completes the statement. *PRINT THE LETTER OF THE CORRECT ANSWER IN THE SPACE AT THE RIGHT.*

1. The plural of 1.___
   A. turkey is turkies
   B. cargo is cargoes
   C. bankruptcy is bankruptcys
   D. son-in-law is son-in-laws

2. The abbreviation *viz.* means MOST NEARLY 2.___
   A. namely   B. for example
   C. the following   D. see

3. In the sentence, *A man in a light-grey suit waited thirty-five minutes in the ante-room for the all-important document*, the word IMPROPERLY hyphenated is 3.___
   A. light-grey   B. thirty-five
   C. ante-room   D. all-important

4. The MOST accurate of the following sentences is: 4.___
   A. The commissioner, as well as his deputy and various bureau heads, were present.
   B. A new organization of employers and employees have been formed.
   C. One or the other of these men have been selected.
   D. The number of pages in the book is enough to discourage a reader.

5. The MOST accurate of the following sentences is: 5.___
   A. Between you and me, I think he is the better man.
   B. He was believed to be me.
   C. Is it us that you wish to see?
   D. The winners are him and her.

Questions 6-13.

DIRECTIONS: The sentences numbered 6 through 13 deal with some phase of police activity. They may be classified most appropriately under one of the following four categories.
   A. Faulty because of incorrect grammar
   B. Faulty because of incorrect punctuation
   C. Faulty because of incorrect use of a word
   D. Correct

Examine each sentence carefully. Then, in the space at the right, print the capital letter preceding the option which is the BEST of the four suggested above. All incorrect sentences contain only one type of error. Consider a sentence correct if it contains none of the types of errors mentioned, even though there may be other correct ways of expressing the same thought.

6. The Department Medal of Honor is awarded to a member of the Police Force who distinguishes himself inconspicuously in the line of police duty by the performance of an act of gallantry. 6.___

7. Members of the Detective Division are charged with the prevention of crime, the detection and arrest of criminals and the recovery of lost or stolen property. 7.___

8. Detectives are selected from the uniformed patrol forces after they have indicated by conduct, aptitude and performance that they are qualified for the more intricate duties of a detective. 8.___

9. The patrolman, pursuing his assailant, exchanged shots with the gunman and immortaly wounded him as he fled into a nearby building. 9.___

10. The members of the Traffic Division has to enforce the Vehicle and Traffic Law, the Traffic Regulations and ordinances relating to vehicular and pedestrian traffic. 10.___

11. After firing a shot at the gunman, the crowd dispersed from the patrolman's line of fire. 11.___

12. The efficiency of the Missing Persons Bureau is maintained with a maximum of public personnel due to the specialized training given to its members. 12.___

13. Records of persons arrested for violations of Vehicle and Traffic Regulations are transmitted upon request to precincts, courts and other authorized agencies. 13.___

14. Following are two sentences which may or may not be written in correct English:
    I. Two clients assaulted the officer.
    II. The van is illegally parked.
    Which one of the following statements is CORRECT?
    A. Only Sentence I is written in correct English.
    B. Only Sentence II is written in correct English.
    C. Sentences I and II are both written in correct English.
    D. Neither Sentence I nor Sentence II is written in correct English. 14.___

15. Following are two sentences which may or may not be written in correct English:
    I. Security Officer Rollo escorted the visitor to the patrolroom.
    II. Two entry were made in the facility logbook. 15.___

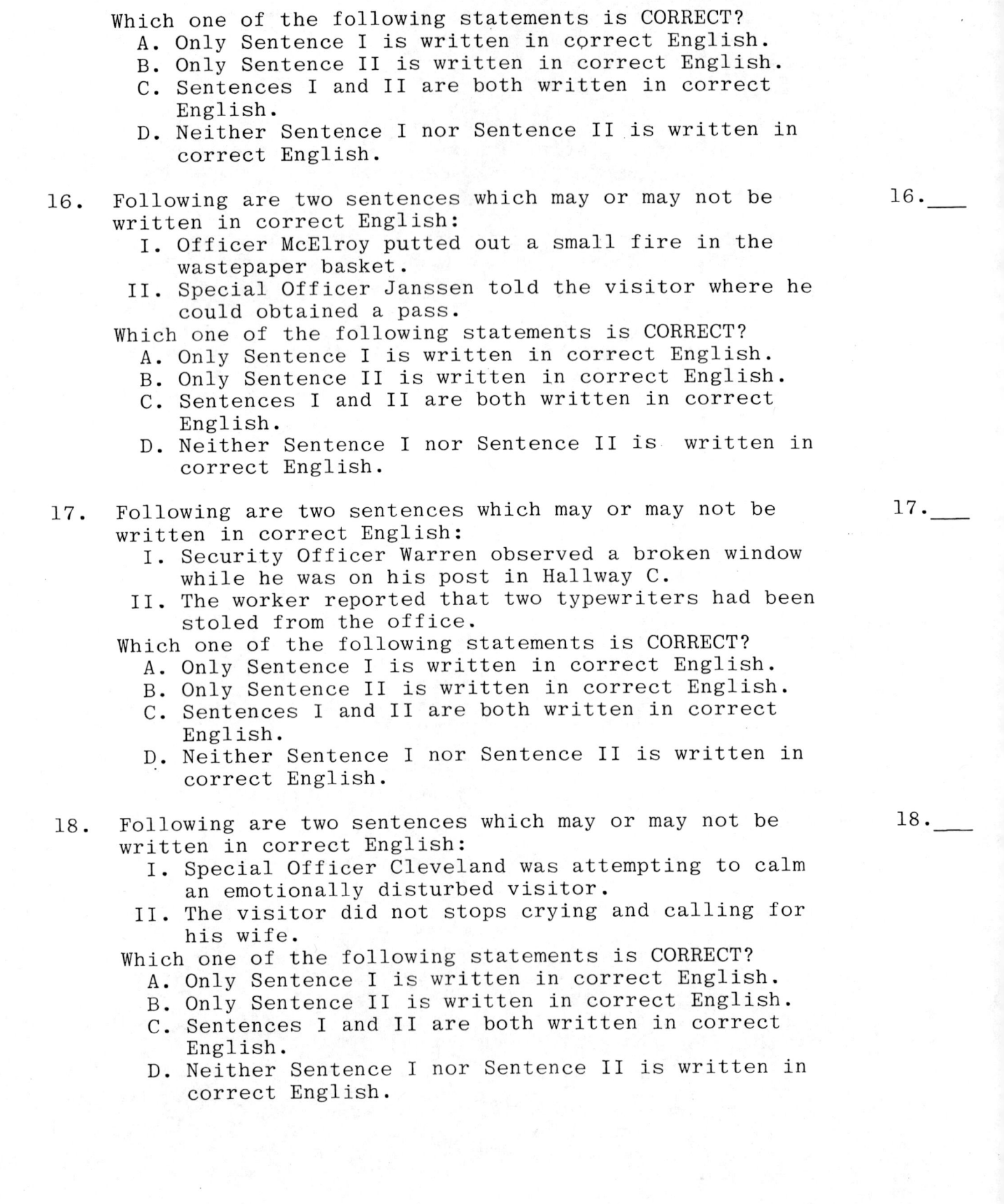

Which one of the following statements is CORRECT?
   A. Only Sentence I is written in correct English.
   B. Only Sentence II is written in correct English.
   C. Sentences I and II are both written in correct English.
   D. Neither Sentence I nor Sentence II is written in correct English.

16. Following are two sentences which may or may not be written in correct English:
   I. Officer McElroy putted out a small fire in the wastepaper basket.
   II. Special Officer Janssen told the visitor where he could obtained a pass.
Which one of the following statements is CORRECT?
   A. Only Sentence I is written in correct English.
   B. Only Sentence II is written in correct English.
   C. Sentences I and II are both written in correct English.
   D. Neither Sentence I nor Sentence II is written in correct English.

17. Following are two sentences which may or may not be written in correct English:
   I. Security Officer Warren observed a broken window while he was on his post in Hallway C.
   II. The worker reported that two typewriters had been stoled from the office.
Which one of the following statements is CORRECT?
   A. Only Sentence I is written in correct English.
   B. Only Sentence II is written in correct English.
   C. Sentences I and II are both written in correct English.
   D. Neither Sentence I nor Sentence II is written in correct English.

18. Following are two sentences which may or may not be written in correct English:
   I. Special Officer Cleveland was attempting to calm an emotionally disturbed visitor.
   II. The visitor did not stops crying and calling for his wife.
Which one of the following statements is CORRECT?
   A. Only Sentence I is written in correct English.
   B. Only Sentence II is written in correct English.
   C. Sentences I and II are both written in correct English.
   D. Neither Sentence I nor Sentence II is written in correct English.

19. Following are two sentences that may or may not be written in correct English:
   I. While on patrol, I observes a vagrant loitering near the drug dispensary.
   II. I escorted the vagrant out of the building and off the premises.
   Which one of the following statements is CORRECT?
   A. Only Sentence I is written in correct English.
   B. Only Sentence II is written in correct English.
   C. Sentences I and II are both written in correct English.
   D. Neither Sentence I nor Sentence II is written in correct English.

19.___

20. Following are two sentences which may or may not be written in correct English:
   I. At 4:00 P.M., Sergeant Raymond told me to evacuate the waiting area immediately due to a bomb threat.
   II. Some of the clients did not want to leave the building.
   Which one of the following statements is CORRECT?
   A. Only Sentence I is written in correct English.
   B. Only Sentence II is written in correct English.
   C. Sentences I and II are both written in correct English.
   D. Neither Sentence I nor Sentence II is written in correct English.

20.___

KEY (CORRECT ANSWERS)

1. B	11. A
2. A	12. C
3. C	13. D
4. D	14. C
5. A	15. A
6. C	16. D
7. B	17. A
8. D	18. A
9. C	19. B
10. A	20. C

PREPARING WRITTEN MATERIAL

PARAGRAPH REARRANGEMENT

COMMENTARY

The sentences which follow are in scrambled order. You are to rearrange them in proper order and indicate the letter choice containing the correct answer at the space at the right.

Each group of sentences in this section is actually a paragraph presented in scrambled order. Each sentence in the group has a place in that paragraph; no sentence is to be left out. You are to read each group of sentences and decide upon the best order in which to put the sentences so as to form as well-organized paragraph.

The questions in this section measure the ability to solve a problem when all the facts relevant to its solution are not given.

More specifically, certain positions of responsibility and authority require the employee to discover connections between events sometimes, apparently, unrelated. In order to do this, the employee will find it necessary to correctly infer that unspecified events have probably occurred or are likely to occur. This ability becomes especially important when action must be taken on incomplete information.

Accordingly, these questions require competitors to choose among several suggested alternatives, each of which presents a different sequential arrangement of the events. Competitors must choose the MOST logical of the suggested sequences.

In order to do so, they may be required to draw on general knowledge to infer missing concepts or events that are essential to sequencing the given events. Competitors should be careful to infer only what is essential to the sequence. The plausibility of the wrong alternatives will always require the inclusion of unlikely events or of additional chains of events which are NOT essential to sequencing the given events.

It's very important to remember that you are looking for the best of the four possible choices, and that the best choice of all may not even be one of the answers you're given to choose from.

There is no one right way to these problems. Many people have found it helpful to first write out the order of the sentences, as they would have arranged them, on their scrap paper before looking at the possible answers. If their optimum answer is there, this can save them some time. If it isn't, this method can still give insight into solving the problem. Others find it most helpful to just go through each of the possible choices, contrasting each as they go along. You should use whatever method feels comfortable, and works, for you.

While most of these types of questions are not that difficult, we've added a higher percentage of the difficult type, just to give you more practice. Usually there are only one or two questions on this section that contain such subtle distinctions that you're unable to answer confidently, and you then may find yourself stuck deciding between two possible choices, neither of which you're sure about.

EXAMINATION SECTION
TEST 1

DIRECTIONS: The following groups of sentences need to be arranged in an order that makes sense. Select the letter preceding the sequence that represents the BEST sentence order. *PRINT THE LETTER OF THE CORRECT ANSWER IN THE SPACE AT THE RIGHT.*

1.
   I. The keyboard was purposely designed to be a little awkward to slow typists down.
   II. The arrangement of letters on the keyboard of a typewriter was not designed for the convenience of the typist.
   III. Fortunately, no one is suggesting that a new keyboard be designed right away.
   IV. If one were, we would have to learn to type all over again.
   V. The reason was that the early machines were slower than the typists and would jam easily.

   A. I, III, IV, II, V   B. II, V, I, IV, III
   C. V, I, II, III, IV   D. II, I, V, III, IV

   1.___

2.
   I. The majority of the new service jobs are part-time or low-paying.
   II. According to the U.S. Bureau of Labor Statistics, jobs in the service sector constitute 72% of all jobs in this country.
   III. If more and more workers receive less and less money, who will buy the goods and services needed to keep the economy going?
   IV. The service sector is by far the fastest growing part of the United States economy.
   V. Some economists look upon this trend with great concern.

   A. II, IV, I, V, III   B. II, III, IV, I, V
   C. V, IV, II, III, I   D. III, I, II, IV, V

   2.___

3.
   I. They can also affect one's endurance.
   II. This can stabilize blood sugar levels, and ensure that the brain is receiving a steady, constant supply of glucose, so that one is *hitting on all cylinders* while taking the test.
   III. By food, we mean real food, not junk food or unhealthy snacks.
   IV. For this reason, it is important not to skip a meal, and to bring food with you to the exam.
   V. One's blood sugar levels can affect how clearly one is able to think and concentrate during an exam.

   A. V, IV, II, III, I   B. V, II, I, IV, III
   C. V, I, IV, III, II   D. V, IV, I, III, II

   3.___

4. I. Those who are the embodiment of desire are absorbed in material quests, and those who are the embodiment of feeling are warriors who value power more than possession.
    II. These qualities are in everyone, but in different degrees.
    III. But those who value understanding yearn not for goods or victory, but for knowledge.
    IV. According to Plato, human behavior flows from three main sources: desire, emotion, and knowledge.
    V. In the perfect state, the industrial forces would produce but not rule, the military would protect but not rule, and the forces of knowledge, the philosopher kings, would reign.

    A. IV, V, I, II, III   B. V, I, II, III, IV
    C. IV, III, II, I, V   D. IV, II, I, III, V

5. I. Of the more than 26,000 tons of garbage produced daily in New York City, 12,000 tons arrive daily at Fresh Kills.
    II. In a month, enough garbage accumulates there to fill the Empire State Building.
    III. In 1937, the Supreme Court halted the practice of dumping the trash of New York City into the sea.
    IV. Although the garbage is compacted, in a few years the mounds of garbage at Fresh Kills will be the highest points south of Maine's Mount Desert Island on the Eastern Seaboard.
    V. Instead, tugboats now pull barges of much of the trash to Staten Island and the largest landfill in the world, Fresh Kills.

    A. III, V, IV, I, II   B. III, V, II, IV, I
    C. III, V, I, II, IV   D. III, II, V, IV, I

6. I. Communists rank equality very high, but freedom very low.
    II. Unlike communists, conservatives place a high value on freedom and a very low value on equality.
    III. A recent study demonstrated that one way to classify people's political beliefs is to look at the importance placed on two words: freedom and equality.
    IV. Thus, by demonstrating how members of these groups feel about the two words, the study has proved to be useful for political analysts in several European countries.
    V. According to the study, socialists and liberals rank both freedom and equality very high, while fascists rate both very low.

    A. III, V, I, II, IV   B. III, IV, V, I, II
    C. III, V, IV, II, I   D. III, I, II, IV, V

7.
    I. "Can there be anything more amazing than this?"
   II. If the riddle is successfully answered, his dead brothers will be brought back to life.
  III. "Even though man sees those around him dying every day," says Dharmaraj, "he still believes and acts as if he were immortal."
  IV. "What is the cause of ceaseless wonder?" asks the Lord of the Lake.
   V. In the ancient epic, The Mahabharata, a riddle is asked of one of the Pandava brothers.

    A. V, II, I, IV, III   B. V, IV, III, I, II
    C. V, II, IV, III, I   D. V, II, IV, I, III

7.___

8.
    I. On the contrary, the two main theories -- the cooperative (neoclassical) theory and the radical (labor theory) -- clearly rest on very different assumptions, which have very different ethical overtones.
  II. The distribution of income is the primary factor in determining the relative levels of material well-being that different groups or individuals attain.
  III. Of all issues in economics, the distribution of income is one of the most controversial.
  IV. The neoclassical theory tends to support the existing income distribution (or minor changes), while the labor theory tends to support substantial changes in the way income is distributed.
   V. The intensity of the controversy reflects the fact that different economic theories are not purely neutral, *detached* theories with no ethical or moral implications.

    A. II, I, V, IV, III   B. III, II, V, I, IV
    C. III, V, II, I, IV   D. III, V, IV, I, II

8.___

9.
    I. The pool acts as a broker and ensures that the cheapest power gets used first.
  II. Every six seconds, the pool's computer monitors all of the generating stations in the state and decides which to ask for more power and which to cut back.
  III. The buying and selling of electrical power is handled by the New York Power Pool in Guilderland, New York.
  IV. This is to the advantage of both the buying and selling utilities.
   V. The pool began operation in 1970, and consists of the state's eight electric utilities.

    A. V, I, II, III, IV   B. IV, II, I, III, V
    C. III, V, I, IV, II   D. V, III, IV, II, I

9.___

10.
  I. Modern English is much simpler grammatically than Old English.
  II. Finnish grammar is very complicated; there are some fifteen cases, for example.
  III. Chinese, a very old language, may seem to be the exception, but it is the great number of characters/words that must be mastered that makes it so difficult to learn, not its grammar.
  IV. The newest literary language -- that is, written as well as spoken -- is Finnish, whose literary roots go back only to about the middle of the nineteenth century.
  V. Contrary to popular belief, the longer a language is been in use the simpler its grammar -- not the reverse.

  A. IV, I, II, III, V   B. V, I, IV, II, III
  C. I, II, IV, III, V   D. IV, II, III, I, V

KEY (CORRECT ANSWERS)

1. D   6. A
2. A   7. C
3. C   8. B
4. D   9. C
5. C   10. B

TEST 2

DIRECTIONS: This type of question tests your ability to recognize accurate paraphrasing, well-constructed paragraphs, and appropriate style and tone. It is important that the answer you select contains only the facts or concepts given in the original sentences. It is also important that you be aware of incomplete sentences, inappropriate transitions, unsupported opinions, incorrect usage, and illogical sentence order. Paragraphs that do not include all the necessary facts and concepts, that distort them, or that add new ones are not considered correct.

The format for this section may vary. Sometimes, long paragraphs are given, and emphasis is placed on style and organization. Our first five questions are of this type. Other times, the paragraphs are shorter, and there is less emphasis on style and more emphasis on accurate representation of information. Our second group of five questions are of this nature.

For each of Questions 1 through 10, select the paragraph that BEST expresses the ideas contained in the sentences above it. *PRINT THE LETTER OF THE CORRECT ANSWER IN THE SPACE AT THE RIGHT.*

1.
    I. Listening skills are very important for managers.
    II. Listening skills are not usually emphasized.
    III. Whenever managers are depicted in books, manuals or the media, they are always talking, never listening.
    IV. We'd like you to read the enclosed handout on listening skills and to try to consciously apply them this week.
    V. We guarantee they will improve the quality of your interactions.

1.___

    A. Unfortunately, listening skills are not usually emphasized for managers. Managers are always depicted as talking, never listening. We'd like you to read the enclosed handout on listening skills. Please try to apply these principles this week. If you do, we guarantee they will improve the quality of your interactions.

    B. The enclosed handout on listening skills will be important improving the quality of your interactions. We guarantee it. All you have to do is take some time this week to read it and to consciously try to apply the principles. Listening skills are very important for managers, but they are not usually emphasized. Whenever managers are depicted in books, manuals or the media, they are always talking, never listening.

C. Listening well is one of the most important skills a manager can have, yet it's not usually given much attention. Think about any representation of managers in books, manuals, or in the media that you may have seen. They're always talking, never listening. We'd like you to read the enclosed handout on listening skills and consciously try to apply them the rest of the week. We guarantee you will see a difference in the quality of your interactions.

D. Effective listening, one very important tool in the effective manager's arsenal, is usually not emphasized enough. The usual depiction of managers in books, manuals or the media is one in which they are always talking, never listening. We'd like you to read the enclosed handout and consciously try to apply the information contained therein throughout the rest of the week. We feel sure that you will see a marked difference in the quality of your interactions.

2.
I. Chekhov wrote three dramatic masterpieces which share certain themes and formats: <u>Uncle Vanya</u>, <u>The Cherry Orchard</u>, and <u>The Three Sisters</u>.
II. They are primarily concerned with the passage of time and how this erodes human aspirations.
III. The plays are haunted by the ghosts of the wasted life.
IV. The characters are concerned with life's lesser problems; however, such as the inability to make decisions, loyalty to the wrong cause, and the inability to be clear.
V. This results in a sweet, almost aching, type of a sadness referred to as Chekhovian.

2.___

A. Chekhov wrote three dramatic masterpieces: <u>Uncle Vanya</u>, <u>The Cherry Orchard</u>, and <u>The Three Sisters</u>. These masterpieces share certain themes and formats: the passage of time, how time erodes human aspirations, and the ghosts of wasted life. Each masterpiece is characterized by a sweet, almost aching, type of sadness that has become known as Chekhovian. The sweetness of this sadness hinges on the fact that it is not the great tragedies of life which are destroying these characters, but their minor flaws: indecisiveness, misplaced loyalty, unclarity.

B. <u>The Cherry Orchard</u>, <u>Uncle Vanya</u>, and <u>The Three Sisters</u> are three dramatic masterpieces written by Chekhov that use similar formats to explore a common theme. Each is primarily concerned with the way that passing time wears down human aspirations, and each is haunted by the ghosts of the wasted life. The characters are shown struggling futilely with the lesser problems of life: indecisiveness, loyalty to the wrong cause, and the inability to be clear. These struggles create a mood of sweet, almost aching, sadness that has become known as Chekhovian.

C. Chekhov's dramatic masterpieces are, along with _The Cherry Orchard_, _Uncle Vanya_, and _The Three Sisters_. These plays share certain thematic and formal similarities. They are concerned most of all with the passage of time and the way in which time erodes human aspirations. Each play is haunted by the specter of the wasted life. Chekhov's characters are caught, however, by life's lesser snares: indecisiveness, loyalty to the wrong cause, and unclarity. The characteristic mood is a sweet, almost aching type of sadness that has come to be known as Chekhovian.

D. A Chekhovian mood is characterized by sweet, almost aching, sadness. The term comes from three dramatic tragedies by Chekhov which revolve around the sadness of a wasted life. The three masterpieces (_Uncle Vanya_, _The Three Sisters_, and _The Cherry Orchard_) share the same theme and format. The plays are concerned with how the passage of time erodes human aspirations. They are peopled with characters who are struggling with life's lesser problems. These are people who are indecisive, loyal to the wrong causes, or are unable to make themselves clear.

3. I. Movie previews have often helped producers decide what parts of movies they should take out or leave in.
    II. The first 1933 preview of _King Kong_ was very helpful to the producers because many people ran screaming from the theater and would not return when four men first attacked by Kong were eaten by giant spiders.
    III. The 1950 premiere of Sunset Boulevard resulted in the filming of an entirely new beginning, and a delay of six months in the film's release.
    IV. In the original opening scene, William Holden was in a morgue talking with thirty-six other "corpses" about the ways some of them had died.
    V. When he began to tell them of his life with Gloria Swanson, the audience found this hilarious, instead of taking the scene seriously.

3. ___

A. Movie previews have often helped producers decide what parts of movies they should leave in or take out. For example, the first preview of _King Kong_ in 1933 was very helpful. In one scene, four men were first attacked by Kong and then eaten by giant spiders. Many members of the audience ran screaming from the theater and would not return. The premiere of the 1950 film _Sunset Boulevard_ was also very helpful. In the original opening scene, William Holden was in a morgue with thirty-six other "corpses," discussing the ways some of them had died. When he began to tell them of his life with Gloria Swanson, the audience found this hilarious. They were supposed to take the scene seriously. The result was a delay of six months in the release of the film while a new beginning was added.

B. Movie previews have often helped producers decide whether they should change various parts of a movie. After the 1933 preview of King Kong, a scene in which four men who had been attacked by Kong were eaten by giant spiders was taken out as many people ran screaming from the theater and would not return. The 1950 premiere of Sunset Boulevard also led to some changes. In the original opening scene, William Holden was in a morgue talking with thirty-six other "corpses" about the ways some of them had died. When he began to tell them of his life with Gloria Swanson, the audience found this hilarious, instead of taking the scene seriously.

C. What do Sunset Boulevard and King Kong have in common? Both show the value of using movie previews to test audience reaction. The first 1933 preview of King Kong showed that a scene showing four men being eaten by giant spiders after having been attacked by Kong was too frightening for many people. They ran screaming from the theater and couldn't be coaxed back. The 1950 premiere of Sunset Boulevard was also a scream, but not the kind the producers intended. The movie opens with William Holden lying in a morgue discussing the ways they had died with thirty-six other "corpses." When he began to tell them of his life with Gloria Swanson, the audience couldn't take him seriously. Their laughter caused a six-month delay while the beginning was rewritten.

D. Producers very often use movie previews to decide if changes are needed. The premiere of Sunset Boulevard in 1950 led to a new beginning and a six-month delay in film release. At the beginning, William Holden and thirty-six other "corpses" discuss the ways some of them died. Rather than taking this seriously, the audience thought it was hilarious when he began to tell them of his life with Gloria Swanson. The first 1933 preview of King Kong was very helpful for its producers because one scene so terrified the audience that many of them ran screaming from the theater and would not return. In this particular scene, four men who had first been attacked by Kong were being eaten by giant spiders.

4.   I. It is common for supervisors to view employees as "things" to be manipulated.   4.___
    II. This approach does not motivate employees, nor does the carrot-and-stick approach because employees often recognize these behaviors and resent them.
   III. Supervisors can change these behaviors by using self-inquiry and persistence.
   IV. The best managers genuinely respect those they work with, are supportive and helpful, and are interested in working as a team with those they supervise.
    V. They disagree with the Golden Rule that says "he or she who has the gold makes the rules."

A. Some managers act as if they think the Golden Rule means "he or she who has the gold makes the rules." They show disrespect to employees by seeing them as "things" to be manipulated. Obviously, this approach does not motivate employees any more than the carrot-and-stick approach motivates them. The employees are smart enough to spot these behaviors and resent them. On the other hand, the managers genuinely respect those they work with, are supportive and helpful, and are interested in working as a team. Self-inquiry and persistence can change even the former type of supervisor into the latter.

B. Many supervisors fall into the trap of viewing employees as "things" to be manipulated, or try to motivate them by using a carrot-and-stick approach. These methods do not motivate employees, who often recognize the behaviors and resent them. Supervisors can change these behaviors, however, by using self-inquiry and persistence. The best managers are supportive and helpful, and have genuine respect for those with whom they work. They are interested in working as a team with those they supervise. To them, the Golden Rule is not "he or she who has the gold makes the rules."

C. Some supervisors see employees as "things" to be used or manipulated using a carrot-and-stick technique. These methods don't work. Employees often see through them and resent them. A supervisor who wants to change may do so. The techniques of self-inquiry and persistence can be used to turn him or her into the type of supervisor who doesn't think the Golden Rule is "he or she who has the gold makes the rules." They may become like the best managers who treat those with whom they work with respect and give them help and support. These are the managers who know how to build a team.

D. Unfortunately, many supervisors act as if their employees are objects whose movements they can position at will. This mistaken belief has the same result as another popular motivational technique -- the carrot-and-stick approach. Both attitudes can lead to the same result -- resentment from those employees who recognize the behaviors for what they are. Supervisors who recognize these behaviors can change through the use of persistence and the use of self-inquiry. It's important to remember that the best managers respect their employees. They readily give necessary help and support and are interested in working as a team with those they supervise. To these managers, the Golden Rule is not "he or she who has the gold makes the rules."

5.
    I. The first half of the nineteenth century produced a group of pessimistic poets -- Byron, De Musset, Heine, Pushkin, and Leopardi.
    II. It also produced a group of pessimistic composers -- Schubert, Chopin, Schumann, and even the later Beethoven.
    III. Above all, in philosophy, there was the profoundly pessimistic philosopher, Schopenhauer.
    IV. The Revolution was dead, the Bourbons were restored, the feudal barons were reclaiming their land, and progress everywhere was being suppressed, as the great age was over.
    V. "I thank God," said Goethe, "that I am not young in so thoroughly finished a world."

    A. "I thank God," said Goethe, "that I am not young in so thoroughly finished a world." The Revolution was dead, the Bourbons were restored, the feudal barons were reclaiming their land, and progress everywhere was being suppressed. The first half of the nineteenth century produced a group of pessimistic poets: Byron, De Musset, Heine, Pushkin, and Leopardi. It also produced pessimistic composers: Schubert, Chopin, Schumann. Although Beethoven came later, he fits into this group, too. Finally and above all, it also produced a profoundly pessimistic philosopher, Schopenhauer. The great age was over.
    B. The first half of the nineteenth century produced a group of pessimistic poets: Byron, De Musset, Heine, Pushkin, and Leopardi. It produced a group of pessimistic composers: Schubert, Chopin, Schumann, and even the later Beethoven. Above all, it produced a profoundly pessimistic philosopher, Schopenhauer. For each of these men, the great age was over. The Revolution was dead, and the Bourbons were restored. The feudal barons were reclaiming their land, and progress everywhere was being suppressed.
    C. The great age was over. The Revolution was dead -- the Bourbons were restored, and the feudal barons were reclaiming their land. Progress everywhere was being suppressed. Out of this climate came a profound pessimism. Poets, like Byron, De Musset, Heine, Pushkin, and Leopardi; composers, like Schubert, Chopin, Schumann, and even the later Beethoven; and, above all, a profoundly pessimistic philosopher, Schopenauer. This pessimism which arose in the first half of the nineteenth century is illustrated by these words of Goethe, "I thank God that I am not young in so thoroughly finished a world."
    D. The first half of the nineteenth century produced a group of pessimistic poets, Byron, De Musset, Heine, Pushkin, and Leopardi -- and a group of pessimistic composers, Schubert, Chopin, Schumann, and the later Beethoven. Above all, it produced a profoundly

pessimistic philosopher, Schopenhauer. The great age was over. The Revolution was dead, the Bourbons were restored, the feudal barons were reclaiming their land, and progress everywhere was being suppressed. "I thank God," said Goethe, "that I am not young in so thoroughly finished a world."

6.
   I. A new manager sometimes may feel insecure about his or her competence in the new position.
  II. The new manager may then exhibit defensive or arrogant behavior towards those one supervises, or the new manager may direct overly flattering behavior toward one's new supervisor.

6.___

   A. Sometimes, a new manager may feel insecure about his or her ability to perform well in this new position. The insecurity may lead him or her to treat others differently. He or she may display arrogant or defensive behavior towards those he or she supervises, or be overly flattering to his or her new supervisor.
   B. A new manager may sometimes feel insecure about his or her ability to perform well in the new position. He or she may then become arrogant, defensive, or overly flattering towards those he or she works with.
   C. There are times when a new manager may be insecure about how well he or she can perform in the new job. The new manager may also behave defensive or act in an arrogant way towards those he or she supervises, or overly flatter his or her boss.
   D. Sometimes, a new manager may feel insecure about his or her ability to perform well in the new position. He or she may then display arrogant or defensive behavior towards those they supervise, or become overly flattering towards their supervisors.

7.
   I. It is possible to eliminate unwanted behavior by bringing it under stimulus control -- tying the behavior to a cue, and then never, or rarely, giving the cue.
  II. One trainer successfully used this method to keep an energetic young porpoise from coming out of her tank whenever she felt like it, which was potentially dangerous.
 III. Her trainer taught her to do it for a reward, in response to a hand signal, and then rarely gave the signal.

7.___

   A. Unwanted behavior can be eliminated by tying the behavior to a cue, and then never, or rarely, giving the cue. This is called stimulus control. One trainer was able to use this method to keep an energetic young porpoise from coming out of her tank by teaching her to come out for a reward in response to a hand signal, and then rarely giving the signal.

B. Stimulus control can be used to eliminate unwanted behavior. In this method, behavior is tied to a cue, and then the cue is rarely, if ever, given. One trainer was able to successfully use stimulus control to keep an energetic young porpoise from coming out of her tank whenever she felt like it -- a potentially dangerous practice. She taught the porpoise to come out for a reward when she gave a hand signal, and then rarely gave the signal.
C. It is possible to eliminate behavior that is undesirable by bringing it under stimulus control by tying behavior to a signal, and then rarely giving the signal. One trainer successfully used this method to keep an energetic young porpoise from coming out of her tank, a potentially dangerous situation. Her trainer taught the porpoise to do it for a reward, in response to a hand signal, and then would rarely give the signal.
D. By using stimulus control, it is possible to eliminate unwanted behavior by tying the behavior to a cue, and then rarely or never give the cue. One trainer was able to use this method to successfully stop a young porpoise from coming out of her tank whenever she felt like it. To curb this potentially dangerous practice, the porpoise was taught by the trainer to come out of the tank for a reward, in response to a hand signal, and then rarely given the signal.

8.
I. There is a great deal of concern over the safety of commercial trucks, caused by their greatly increased role in serious accidents since federal deregulation in 1981.
II. Recently, 60 percent of trucks in New York and Connecticut and 70 percent of trucks in Maryland randomly stopped by state troopers failed safety inspections.
III. Sixteen states in the United States require no training at all for truck drivers.

A. Since federal deregulation in 1981, there has been a great deal of concern over the safety of commercial trucks, and their greatly increased role in serious accidents. Recently, 60 percent of trucks in New York and Connecticut, and 70 percent of trucks in Maryland failed safety inspections. Sixteen states in the United States require no training at all for truck drivers.
B. There is a great deal of concern over the safety of commercial trucks since federal deregulation in 1981. Their role in serious accidents has greatly increased. Recently, 60 percent of trucks randomly stopped in Connecticut and New York, and 70 percent in Maryland failed safety inspections conducted by state troopers. Sixteen states in the United States provide no training at all for truck drivers.

C. Commercial trucks have a greatly increased role in serious accidents since federal deregulation in 1981. This has led to a great deal of concern. Recently, 70 percent of trucks in Maryland and 60 percent of trucks in New York and Connecticut failed inspection of those that were randomly stopped by state troopers. Sixteen states in the United States require no training for all truck drivers.

D. Since federal deregulation in 1981, the role that commercial trucks have played in serious accidents has greatly increased, and this has led to a great deal of concern. Recently, 60 percent of trucks in New York and Connecticut, and 70 percent of trucks in Maryland randomly stopped by state troopers failed safety inspections. Sixteen states in the U.S. don't require any training for truck drivers.

9.
I. No matter how much some people have, they still feel unsatisfied and want more, or want to keep what they have forever.
II. One recent television documentary showed several people flying from New York to Paris for a one-day shopping spree to buy platinum earrings, because they were bored.
III. In Brazil, some people are ordering coffins that cost a minimum of $45,000 and are equipping them with deluxe stereos, televisions and other graveyard necessities.

A. Some people, despite having a great deal, still feel unsatisfied and want more, or think they can keep what they have forever. One recent documentary on television showed several people enroute from Paris to New York for a one day shopping spree to buy platinum earrings, because they were bored. Some people in Brazil are even ordering coffins equipped with such graveyard necessities as deluxe stereos and televisions. The price of the coffins start at $45,000.

B. No matter how much some people have, they may feel unsatisfied. This leads them to want more, or to want to keep what they have forever. Recently, a television documentary depicting several people flying from New York to Paris for a one day shopping spree to buy platinum earrings. They were bored. Some people in Brazil are ordering coffins that cost at least $45,000 and come equipped with deluxe televisions, stereos and other necessary graveyard items.

C. Some people will be dissatisfied no matter how much they have. They may want more, or they may want to keep what they have forever. One recent television documentary showed several people, motivated by boredom, jetting from New York to Paris for a one-day shopping spree to buy platinum earrings. In Brazil, some people are ordering coffins equipped with deluxe stereos, televisions and other graveyard necessities. The minimum price for these coffins - $45,000.

10 (#2)

D. Some people are never satisfied. No matter how much they have they still want more, or think they can keep what they have forever. One television documentary recently showed several people flying from New York to Paris for the day to buy platinum earrings because they were bored. In Brazil, some people are ordering coffins that cost $45,000 and are equipped with deluxe stereos, televisions and other graveyard necessities.

10.   I. A television signal or video signal has three parts.   10.___
    II. Its parts are the black-and-white portion, the color portion, and the synchronizing (sync) pulses, which keep the picture stable.
    III. Each video source, whether it's a camera or a video-cassette recorder, contains its own generator of these synchronizing pulses to accompany the picture that it's sending in order to keep it steady and straight.
    IV. In order to produce a clean recording, a video-cassette recorder must "lock-up" to the sync pulses that are part of the video it is trying to record, and this effort may be very noticeable if the device does not have genlock.

    A. There are three parts to a television or video signal: the black-and-white part, the color part, and the synchronizing (sync) pulses, which keep the picture stable. Whether it's a video-cassette recorder or a camera, each each video source contains its own pulse that synchronizes and generates the picture it's sending in order to keep it straight and steady. A video-cassette recorder must "lock up" to the sync pulses that are part of the video it's trying to record. If the device doesn't have genlock, this effort must be very noticeable.
    B. A video signal or television is comprised of three parts: the black-and-white portion, the color portion, and the the sync (synchronizing) pulses, which keep the picture stable. Whether it's a camera or a video-cassette recorder, each video source contains its own generator of these synchronizing pulses. These accompany the picture that it's sending in order to keep it straight and steady. A video-cassette recorder must "lock up" to the sync pulses that are part of the video it is trying to record in order to produce a clean recording. This effort may be very noticeable if the device does not have genlock.
    C. There are three parts to a television or video signal: the color portion, the black-and-white portion, and the sync (synchronizing pulses). These keep the picture stable. Each video source, whether it's a video-cassette recorder or a camera, generates these synchronizing pulses accompanying the picture it's

sending in order to keep it straight and steady. If a clean recording is to be produced, a video-cassette recorder must store the sync pulses that are part of the video it is trying to record. This effort may not be noticeable if the device does not have genlock.
D. A television signal or video signal has three parts: the black-and-white portion, the color portion, and the synchronizing (sync) pulses. It's the sync pulses which keep the picture stable, which accompany it and keep it steady and straight. Whether it's a camera or a video-cassette recorder, each video source contains its own generator of these synchronizing pulses. To produce a clean recording, a video-cassette recorder must "lock-up" to the sync pulses that are part of the video it is trying to record. If the device does not have genlock, this effort may be very noticeable.

KEY (CORRECT ANSWERS)

1. C	6. A
2. B	7. B
3. A	8. D
4. B	9. C
5. D	10. D

READING COMPREHENSION
UNDERSTANDING AND INTERPRETING WRITTEN MATERIAL
EXAMINATION SECTION
TEST 1

Questions 1-10.

DIRECTIONS: Each question or incomplete statement is followed by several suggested answers or completions. Select the one that BEST answers the question or completes the statement. *PRINT THE LETTER OF THE CORRECT ANSWER IN THE SPACE AT THE RIGHT.*

1. Accident prevention is an activity which depends for success upon factual information, research, and analysis. Experience has proved that all accidents can be prevented through the correct application of basic accident prevention methods and techniques determined from factual cause data.
Therefore, to achieve the maximum results from any safety and health program, a uniform system for the reporting of accidents and causes is established. The procedures required for a report, when properly carried out, will determine accurate cause factors and the most practical methods for applying preventive or remedial action.
According to the above paragraphs, which of the following statements is MOST NEARLY correct?
   A. No matter how much effort is put forth, there are some accidents that cannot be prevented.
   B. Accident prevention is a research activity.
   C. Accident reporting systems are not related to accident prevention.
   D. The success of an accident prevention program depends on the correct use of a uniform accident reporting system.

1.___

Questions 2-7.

DIRECTIONS: Questions 2 through 7 are to be answered ONLY according to the information given in the following accident report.

DATE: February 2

TO: Edward Moss, Superintendent
Pacific Houses
2487 Shell Road
Auburnsville, Illinois

SUBJECT: Report of Accident to
Philip Fay, Employee
1825 North 8th St.
Auburnsville, Ill.
Identification #374-24

Philip Fay, an employee, came to my office at 10:15 A.M. yesterday and told me that he hurt his left elbow. When I asked him what happened, he told me that 15 minutes ago, while shoveling the snow from in front of Building #14 at 2280 Stone Ave., he slipped on some snow-covered ice and fell on his elbow. Joseph Sanchez and Arthur Campbell, who were working with him, saw what happened.

Mr. Fay complained of pain and could not bend his left arm. I called for an ambulance right away. A police patrol car from the 85th Precinct arrived 15 minutes later, and Patrolman Johnson, Shield #8743, said that an ambulance was on the way. At 10:45 A.M., an ambulance arrived from Auburn Hospital. Dr. Breen examined Mr. Fay and told me that he would have to go to the hospital for some x-ray pictures to determine how bad the injury was. The ambulance left with Mr. Fay at 11:00 A.M.

At 3:45 P.M., Mr. Fay called from the hospital and told me that his arm had been put in a cast in the emergency room of the hospital. He was told that he had fractured his left elbow and would have to stay out of work for about four weeks. He is to report back at the hospital in three weeks for another examination and to see if the cast can be taken off. His wife was at the hospital with him, and they were now going home.

Attached are the statements from the witnesses and our completed REPORT OF INJURY form.

          William Fields
          Foreman

2. Which one of the following did NOT see the accident?
 A. Campbell B. Fay C. Fields D. Sanchez

3. The CORRECT date and time of accident is February
 A. 2, 10:00 A.M. B. 2, 10:15 A.M.
 C. 1, 10:00 A.M. D. 1, 10:15 A.M.

4. The ambulance came about ____ hour after ____.
 A. $\frac{1}{4}$; the accident B. $\frac{1}{4}$; it was called
 C. $\frac{1}{2}$; the accident D. $\frac{1}{2}$; it was called

5. It is not possible to tell whether Fay went to report the accident right away because the report does NOT say
 A. how long it takes to get from Building #14 to the foreman's office
 B. how long it takes to get from Stone Ave. to Shell Rd.
 C. whether Fay telephoned the foreman first
 D. whether the foreman was in his office as soon as Fay got there

6. From the facts in the report, Fay's action might be criticized because he
 A. did not give the foreman the complete story of what had happened
 B. did not take Campbell or Sanchez with him when he went to the foreman's office in case he should need help on the way
 C. did not remain at the accident site and send Sanchez and Campbell to bring the foreman
 D. telephoned from the hospital and by using his arm to do this he might have aggravated his condition

7. Assuming that the report gives the complete story of this 7.___
incident, the action of the foreman may be criticized
because he did NOT
   A. call an ambulance soon enough
   B. go to the hospital with the ambulance and stay with
the injured man until he was discharged
   C. have the injured man sign a release of claim against
the department
   D. make an on-the-spot investigation of the accident
scene nor take corrective action

Questions 8-10.

DIRECTIONS: Questions 8 through 10 are to be answered ONLY according to the information given in the following passage.

   A foreman has four maintainers and two helpers assigned to him. Listed below are the maintainers and helpers and their rate of speed in completing the assignments given to them. Assume all the foreman's men (maintainers and helpers) are of equal technical ability but some work faster than others while some are slower in completing their assignments. In all cases, no overtime is to be granted.

  Maintainer E - works at average rate of speed
  Maintainer F - works at twice the rate of speed as Maintainer E
  Maintainer G - works at the same rate of speed as Maintainer E
  Maintainer H - works at half the rate of speed as Maintainer E
  Helper J - works at same rate of speed as Maintainer G
  Helper K - works at same rate of speed as Maintainer H

8. A certain job must be done immediately, and Maintainer H 8.___
and Helper J are the only men available.
If Maintainer F, working alone, could normally complete
this job in six days, the TOTAL time this foreman should
allot to Maintainer H and Helper J to complete the same
job is ____ days.
   A. 3   B. 4   C. 8   D. 12

9. While Maintainer E and Helper J are working on a job, 9.___
Helper J reports that he will be out sick for at least
a week. The job normally would have taken four more days
to complete, and it must be completed within these four
days.
If Maintainer H and Helper K are the only two men available,
this foreman should
   A. assign Helper K to replace Helper J
   B. assign Maintainer H to replace Helper J
   C. assign both Maintainer H and Helper K to replace
Helper J
   D. inform his assistant supervisor that the job cannot
be completed on time

10. This foreman has assigned all six of his men to a routine   10.___
    maintenance job. At the end of two days, the job is four-
    fifths completed; and instead of reassigning all his men
    the following day when they would finish early, the foreman
    cuts the gang so that the job will take one more full day
    to finish.
    The work gang on the last day should consist of Maintainer(s)
       A. F and H   B. F and Helper J
       C. E and Helpers J and K   D. G and H and Helper K

Questions 11-25.

DIRECTIONS: Each question consists of a statement. You are to
             indicate whether the statement is TRUE (T) or FALSE (F).
             *PRINT THE LETTER OF THE CORRECT ANSWER IN THE SPACE AT
             THE RIGHT.*

Questions 11-15.

DIRECTIONS: Questions 11 through 15 are to be answered ONLY according
             to the information given in the following paragraph.

USING LADDERS

All ladders must be checked each day for any defects before they are used. They should not be used if there are split rails or loose rungs or if they have become shaky. Two men should handle a stepladder which is over eight feet in height, one man if the ladder is smaller. One man must face the ladder and hold it with a firm grasp while the other is working on it. When you climb a ladder, always face it, grasp the siderails, and climb up one rung at a time. You should come down the same way.

11. A ladder which is new does not have to be inspected before   11.___
    it is used.

12. A ladder with a loose rung may be used if this rung is not   12.___
    stepped on.

13. A stepladder 6 feet long may be handled by one man.   13.___

14. If a 10-foot stepladder is used, one man must hold the   14.___
    ladder while the other works on it.

15. The siderails of a ladder do not have to be held when   15.___
    climbing down.

Questions 16-20.

DIRECTIONS: Questions 16 through 20 are to be answered ONLY according
             to the information given in the following paragraph.

TRAFFIC ACCIDENTS

Three auto accidents happened at the corner of Fifth Street and Seventh Avenue. The first, at 7:00 P.M. last night, knocked down a light pole when two cars collided. At 8:15 A.M. this morning, two other autos crashed head on. This afternoon, at 12:30 P.M., another pair of cars crashed. One of them jumped the curb, knocked over two traffic signs, and damaged three parked cars at the corner service station. No serious injury to the drivers was reported, but all the cars involved were severely damaged.

16. Nine cars were damaged in the three accidents. 16.___

17. The three accidents happened within a period of 14 hours. 17.___

18. A service station is located at the corner of Fifth Street and Seventh Avenue. 18.___

19. In the last accident, both cars jumped the curb and knocked over two light poles. 19.___

20. The drivers of the cars in the last accident were badly hurt. 20.___

Questions 21-25.

DIRECTIONS: Questions 21 through 25 are to be answered ONLY according to the information given in the following paragraph.

LIFTING

Improper lifting of heavy objects is a frequent cause of strains and ruptures. When a heavy object is to be lifted, an employee should stand close to the object and face it squarely. The feet are spread slightly apart, and one foot is a little ahead of the other. Then, bend the knees to bring the body down to the object and keep your back comfortably vertical. Raise the object slightly to see if you can lift it alone. If you can, get a firm grasp with both hands, balance the object, and raise it by straightening the legs, but still keeping the back erect. The raising motion is gradual, not swift. In this way you use the leg muscles which are the strongest muscles in the body. This method of lifting prevents strain to the back muscles which are weak and not built for lifting purposes.

21. Many ruptures are the result of not lifting heavy objects in the correct manner. 21.___

22. When an employee lifts a heavy package, he should keep his feet close together in order to balance the load. 22.___

23. When lifting a heavy object, the back should not be bent but kept upright. 23.___

24. It is best to lift heavy objects quickly in order to prevent strains and ruptures. 24.___

25. For purposes of lifting, the leg muscles are stronger than the arm muscles. 25.___

KEY (CORRECT ANSWERS)

1. D
2. C
3. C
4. D
5. A

6. B
7. D
8. C
9. C
10. B

11. F
12. F
13. T
14. T
15. F

16. T
17. F
18. T
19. F
20. F

21. T
22. F
23. T
24. F
25. T

TEST 2

DIRECTIONS: Each question or incomplete statement is followed by several suggested answers or completions. Select the one that BEST answers the question or completes the statement. *PRINT THE LETTER OF THE CORRECT ANSWER IN THE SPACE AT THE RIGHT.*

Questions 1-8.

DIRECTIONS: Questions 1 through 8, inclusive, are based on the ladder safety rules given below. Read these rules fully before answering these questions.

LADDER SAFETY RULES

When a ladder is placed on a slightly uneven supporting surface, use a flat piece of board or small wedge to even up the ladder feet. To secure the proper angle for resting a ladder, it should be placed so that the distance from the base of the ladder to the supporting wall is one-quarter the length of the ladder. To avoid overloading a ladder, only one person should work on a ladder at a time. Do not place a ladder in front of a door. When the top rung of a ladder rests against a pole, the ladder should be lashed securely. Clear loose stones or debris from the ground around the base of a ladder before climbing. While on a ladder, do not attempt to lean so that any part of the body, except arms or hands, extends more than 12 inches beyond the side rail. Always face the ladder when ascending or descending. When carrying ladders through buildings, watch for ceiling globes and lighting fixtures. Avoid the use of rolling ladders as scaffold supports.

1. A small wedge is used to
   A. even up the feet of a ladder resting on an uneven surface
   B. lock the wheels of a roller ladder
   C. secure the proper resting angle for a ladder
   D. secure a ladder against a pole

2. An 8-foot ladder resting against a wall should be so inclined that the distance between the base of the ladder and the wall is ____ feet.
   A. 2   B. 5   C. 7   D. 9

3. A ladder should be lashed securely when
   A. it is placed in front of a door
   B. loose stones are on the ground near the base of the ladder
   C. the top rung rests against a pole
   D. two people are working from the same ladder

1.____

2.____

3.____

4. Rolling ladders
   A. should be used for scaffold supports
   B. should not be used for scaffold supports
   C. are useful on uneven ground
   D. should be used against a pole

5. When carrying a ladder through a building, it is necessary to
   A. have two men to carry it
   B. carry the ladder vertically
   C. watch for ceiling globes
   D. face the ladder while carrying it

6. It is POOR practice to
   A. lash a ladder securely at any time
   B. clear debris from the base of a ladder before climbing
   C. even up the feet of a ladder resting on slightly uneven ground
   D. place a ladder in front of a door

7. A person on a ladder should NOT extend his head beyond the side rail by more than ____ inches.
   A. 12   B. 9   C. 7   D. 5

8. The MOST important reason for permitting only one person to work on a ladder at a time is that
   A. both could not face the ladder at one time
   B. the ladder will be overloaded
   C. time would be lost going up and down the ladder
   D. they would obstruct each other

Questions 9-13.

DIRECTIONS: Questions 9 through 13 concern an excerpt of written material which you are to read and study carefully. The excerpt is immediately followed by five statements which refer to it alone. You are required to judge whether each statement
   A. is entirely true
   B. is entirely false
   C. is partly true and partly false
   D. may or may not be true but cannot be answered on the basis of the facts as given in the excerpt

It is true that in 1987 there were more strikes than in any year, excepting 1986, since 1970. However, the number of workers involved was less in 1987 than in any year since 1981, and man-days of idleness due to strikes, the MOST accurate measure of industrial strife, were less in 1987 than in any year since 1980, again excepting 1986.

9. There were fewer workers involved in strikes in 1986 than in 1981.

10. There were more strikes in 1986 than in 1987.

11. There were more strikes in 1986 than in 1970.   11.____

12. There were fewer workers involved in strikes but more   12.____
    man-days of idleness in 1981 than 1987.

13. There were fewer man-days of idleness and fewer workers   13.____
    involved in strikes in 1986 than 1987.

Questions 14-16.

DIRECTIONS: Questions 14 through 16 are to be answered on the basis
             of the information given in the following passage.

   Telephone service in a government agency should be adequate and
complete with respect to information given or action taken. It must
be remembered that telephone contacts should receive special consideration since the caller cannot see the operator. People like to
feel that they are receiving personal attention and that their
requests or criticisms are receiving individual rather than routine
consideration. All this contributes to what has come to be known as
Tone of Service. The aim is to use standards which are clearly very
good or superior. The factors to be considered in determining what
makes good Tone of Service are speech, courtesy, understanding, and
explanations. A caller's impression of Tone of Service will affect
the general attitude toward the agency and city services in general.

14. The above passage states that people who telephone a   14.____
    government agency like to feel that they are
      A. creating a positive image of themselves
      B. being given routine consideration
      C. receiving individual attention
      D. setting standards for telephone service

15. Which of the following is NOT mentioned in the above   15.____
    passage as a factor in determining good Tone of Service?
      A. Courtesy   B. Education
      C. Speech   D. Understanding

16. The above passage IMPLIES that failure to properly   16.____
    handle telephone calls is *most likely* to result in
      A. a poor impression of city agencies by the public
      B. a deterioration of courtesy toward operators
      C. an effort by operators to improve the Tone of Service
      D. special consideration by the public of operator
         difficulties

Questions 17-20.

DIRECTIONS: Questions 17 through 20 are to be answered ONLY according
             to the information given in the following passage.

ACCIDENT PREVENTION

   Many accidents and injuries can be prevented if employees learn
to be more careful. The wearing of shoes with thin or badly worn
soles or open toes can easily lead to foot injuries from tacks, nails,
and chair and desk legs. Loose or torn clothing should not be worn
near moving machinery. This is especially true of neckties which

can very easily become caught in the machine. You should not place objects so that they block or partly block hallways, corridors, or other passageways. Even when they are stored in the proper place, tools, supplies, and equipment should be carefully placed or piled so as not to fall, nor have anything stick out from a pile. Before cabinets, lockers or ladders are moved, the tops should be cleared of anything which might injure someone or fall off. If necessary, use a dolly to move these or other bulky objects.

Despite all efforts to avoid accidents and injuries, however, some will happen. If an employee is injured, no matter how small the injury, he should report it to his supervisor and have the injury treated. A small cut that is not attended to can easily become infected and can cause more trouble than some injuries which at first seem more serious. It never pays to take chances.

17. According to the above passage, the one statement that is NOT true is that
    A. by being more careful, employees can reduce the number of accidents that happen
    B. women should wear shoes with open toes for comfort when working
    C. supplies should be piled so that nothing is sticking out from the pile
    D. if an employee sprains his wrist at work, he should tell his supervisor about it

17.____

18. According to the above passage, you should NOT wear loose clothing when you are
    A. in a corridor   B. storing tools
    C. opening cabinets   D. near moving machinery

18.____

19. According to the above passage, before moving a ladder you should
    A. test all the rungs
    B. get a dolly to carry the ladder at all times
    C. remove everything from the top of the ladder which might fall off
    D. remove your necktie

19.____

20. According to the above passage, an employee who gets a slight cut should
    A. have it treated to help prevent infection
    B. know that a slight cut becomes more easily infected than a big cut
    C. pay no attention to it as it can't become serious
    D. realize that it is more serious than any other type of injury

20.____

Questions 21-24.

DIRECTIONS: Questions 21 through 24 are to be answered on the basis of the following report.

TO: Thomas Smith
Supervising Menagerie Keeper

Date: June 14

Subject:

FROM: Jay Jones
Senior Menagerie Keeper

On June 14, a visitor to the monkey house at the zoo was noticed annoying the animals. He was frightening the animals by making loud noises and throwing stones at the animals in the cages. The visitor was asked to stop annoying the animals but did not. And he was then asked to leave the monkey house by the keeper on duty. The visitor would not leave and said that the zoo is public property and that as a citizen he has every right to be there. The keeper kept trying to pursuade the visitor to leave but was unsuccessful. The keeper finally threatened to call the police. The visitor soon left the monkey house and did not return. Fortunately, no animals were harmed in this incident.

21. The subject of the report has been left out. Which one of these would be the BEST statement for the subject of the report?
    A. Loud noises in the monkey house
    B. Police called to monkey house
    C. Visitor annoying monkeys on June 14
    D. Monkeys unharmed by visitor

22. Which one of these is an important piece of information that should have been included in the FIRST sentence of the report?
    A. The kinds of monkeys in the monkey house
    B. Whether the visitor was a man or a woman
    C. The address of the monkey house
    D. The name of the zoo where the incident took place

23. The fourth sentence which begins with the words *And he was then asked*... is poorly written because
    A. the sentence begins with *And*
    B. the words *monkey house* should be written *Monkey House*
    C. the words *on duty* should be written *on-duty*
    D. *didn't* would be better than *did not*

24. In the sixth sentence, which begins with the words *The keeper kept trying*..., a word that is spelled wrong is
    A. trying   B. pursuade
    C. visitor   D. unsuccessful

Questions 25-27.

DIRECTIONS: Questions 25 through 27 test how well you can read and understand what you read. Read about ELEPHANTS. Then, on the basis of what you read, answer these questions.

ELEPHANTS

Elephants are peaceful animals and have very few real natural enemies. As with many other animals, when faced with danger the elephant tries to make himself look larger to his enemy. He does this by raising his head and trunk to look taller. The elephant will also extend his ears to look wider. Other threatening gestures may be made. The elephant may shift his weight from side to side, make a shrill scream, or pretend to charge with his trunk held high. If the enemy still fails to retreat, the elephant will make a serious attack.

25. When an elephant is in danger, he tries to make it appear that he is
    A. stronger   B. smaller   C. larger   D. angry

26. When he is threatened, an elephant tries to make himself look broader by
    A. taking a deep breath
    B. spreading out his ears
    C. shifting his weight from side to side
    D. holding his trunk high

27. If his enemy does not run away, the elephant will
    A. attack him
    B. run in the opposite direction
    C. hit the enemy with his trunk
    D. make a shrill scream

Questions 28-30.

DIRECTIONS: Read about PREVENTING DISEASE. Then, on the basis of what you read, answer Questions 28 through 30.

PREVENTING DISEASE

Proper feeding, housing, and handling are important in maintaining an animal's defenses against disease and parasites. The best diets are those that contain proteins, vitamins, minerals, and the other essential food elements. Proteins are especially important because they are necessary for growth. Minerals such as iron, copper, and cobalt help correct anemia. It has been shown that an animal's resistance can be decreased by improper feeding. However, it has not been proved that the use of certain types of feeds will increase the resistance of animals to infectious diseases. If animals are kept in good condition by proper diet and sanitary conditions, natural resistance to disease and parasites will be highest.

28. Food elements that are required especially for growth   28.___
    are
    A. minerals   B. vitamins
    C. proteins   D. carbohydrates

29. If animals are NOT fed correctly, they will   29.___
    A. have more diseases
    B. fight with each other
    C. need more proteins
    D. be able to kill parasites

30. The bodies of animals will BEST be able to fight disease   30.___
    naturally when they
    A. are kept warm
    B. are given immunity shots
    C. are given extra food
    D. have good diet and clean quarters

KEY (CORRECT ANSWERS)

1. A	11. D	21. C
2. A	12. A	22. D
3. C	13. C	23. A
4. B	14. C	24. B
5. C	15. B	25. C
6. D	16. A	26. B
7. A	17. B	27. A
8. B	18. D	28. C
9. B	19. C	29. A
10. A	20. A	30. D

EXAMINATION SECTION

TEST 1

DIRECTIONS: Each question or incomplete statement is followed by several suggested answers or completions. Select the one that BEST answers the question or completes the statement. *PRINT THE LETTER OF THE CORRECT ANSWER IN THE SPACE AT THE RIGHT.*

1. Of the following, the one MOST important quality required of a good supervisor is
    A. ambition
    B. leadership
    C. friendliness
    D. popularity

   1.____

2. It is often said that a supervisor can delegate authority but never responsibility.
   This means MOST NEARLY that
    A. a supervisor must do his own work if he expects it to be done properly
    B. a supervisor can assign someone else to do his work, but in the last analysis, the supervisor himself must take the blame for any actions followed
    C. authority and responsibility are two separate things that cannot be borne by the same person
    D. it is better for a supervisor never to delegate his authority

   2.____

3. One of your men who is a habitual complainer asks you to grant him a minor privilege.
   Before granting or denying such a request, you should consider
    A. the merits of the case
    B. that it is good for group morale to grant a request of this nature
    C. the man's seniority
    D. that to deny such a request will lower your standing with the men

   3.____

4. A supervisory practice on the part of a foreman which is MOST likely to lead to confusion and inefficiency is for him to
    A. give orders verbally directly to the man assigned to the job
    B. issue orders only in writing
    C. follow up his orders after issuing them
    D. relay his orders to the men through co-workers

   4.____

5. It would be POOR supervision on a foreman's part if he
    A. asked an experienced maintainer for his opinion on the method of doing a special job
    B. make it a policy to avoid criticizing a man in front of his co-workers
    C. consulted his assistant supervisor on unusual problems
    D. allowed a cooling-off period of several days before giving one of his men a deserved reprimand

   5.____

6. Of the following behavior characteristics of a supervisor, the one that is MOST likely to lower the morale of the men he supervises is
   A. diligence
   B. favoritism
   C. punctuality
   D. thoroughness

7. Of the following, the BEST method of getting an employee who is not working up to his capacity to produce more work is to
   A. have another employee criticize his production
   B. privately criticize his production but encourage him to produce more
   C. criticize his production before his associates
   D. criticize his production and threaten to fire him

8. Of the following, the BEST thing for a supervisor to do when a subordinate has done a very good job is to
   A. tell him to take it easy
   B. praise his work
   C. reduce his workload
   D. say nothing because he may become conceited

9. Your orders to your crew are MOST likely to be followed if you
   A. explain the reasons for these orders
   B. warn that all violators will be punished
   C. promise easy assignments to those who follow these orders best
   D. say that they are for the good of the department

10. In order to be a good supervisor, you should
    A. impress upon your men that you demand perfection in their work at all times
    B. avoid being blamed for your crew's mistakes
    C. impress your superior with your ability
    D. see to it that your men get what they are entitled to

11. In giving instructions to a crew, you should
    A. speak in as loud a tone as possible
    B. speak in a coaxing, persuasive manner
    C. speak quietly, clearly, and courteously
    D. always use the word *please* when giving instructions

12. Of the following factors, the one which is LEAST important in evaluating an employee and his work is his
    A. dependability
    B. quantity of work done
    C. quality of work done
    D. education and training

13. When a District Superintendent first assumes his command, it is LEAST important for him at the beginning to observe
    A. how his equipment is designed and its adaptability
    B. how to reorganize the district for greater efficiency
    C. the capabilities of the men in the district
    D. the methods of operation being employed

14. When making an inspection of one of the buildings under 14.____
your supervision, the BEST procedure to follow in making
a record of the inspection is to
    A. return immediately to the office and write a report
       from memory
    B. write down all the important facts during or as soon
       as you complete the inspection
    C. fix in your mind all important facts so that you can
       repeat them from memory if necessary
    D. fix in your mind all important facts so that you can
       make out your report at the end of the day

15. Assume that your superior has directed you to make certain 15.____
changes in your established procedure. After using this
modified procedure on several occasions, you find that the
original procedure was distinctly superior and you wish to
return to it.
You should
    A. let your superior find this out for himself
    B. simply change back to the original procedure
    C. compile definite data and information to prove your
       case to your superior
    D. persuade one of the more experienced workers to take
       this matter up with your superior

16. An inspector visited a large building under construction. 16.____
He inspected the soil lines at 9 A.M., water lines at
10 A.M., fixtures at 11 A.M., and did his office work in
the afternoon. He followed the same pattern daily for
weeks.
This procedure was
    A. *good*; because it was methodical and he did not miss
       anything
    B. *good*; because it gave equal time to all phases of the
       plumbing
    C. *bad*; because not enough time was devoted to fixtures
    D. *bad*; because the tradesmen knew when the inspection
       would occur

17. Assume that one of the foremen in a training course, 17.____
which you are conducting, proposes a poor solution for a
maintenance problem.
Of the following, the BEST course of action for you to
take is to
    A. accept the solution tentatively and correct it during
       the next class meeting
    B. point out all the defects of this proposed solution
       and wait until somebody thinks of a better solution
    C. try to get the class to reject this proposed solution
       and develop a better solution
    D. let the matter pass since somebody will present a
       better solution as the class work proceeds

18. As a supervisor, you should be seeking ways to improve the efficiency of shop operations by means such as changing established work procedures.
The following are offered as possible actions that you should consider in changing established work procedures:
   I. Make changes only when your foremen agree to them
   II. Discuss changes with your supervisor before putting them into practice
   III. Standardize any operation which is performed on a continuing basis
   IV. Make changes quickly and quietly in order to avoid dissent
   V. Secure expert guidance before instituting unfamiliar procedures

   Of the following suggested answers, the one that describes the actions to be taken to change established work procedures is
   A. I, IV, and V *only*
   B. II, III, and V *only*
   C. III, IV, and V *only*
   D. All of the above

19. A supervisor determined that a foreman, without informing his superior, delegated responsibility for checking time cards to a member of his gang. The supervisor then called the foreman into his office where he reprimanded the foreman.
This action of the supervisor in reprimanding the foreman was
   A. *proper*; because the checking of time cards is the foreman's responsibility and should not be delegated
   B. *proper*; because the foreman did not ask the supervisor for permission to delegate responsibility
   C. *improper*; because the foreman may no longer take the initiative in solving future problems
   D. *improper*; because the supervisor is interfering in a function which is not his responsibility

20. A capable supervisor should check all operations under his control.
Of the following, the LEAST important reason for doing this is to make sure that
   A. operations are being performed as scheduled
   B. he personally observes all operations at all times
   C. all the operations are still needed
   D. his manpower is being utilized efficiently

21. A supervisor makes it a practice to apply fair and firm discipline in all cases of rule infractions, including those of a minor nature.
This practice should PRIMARILY be considered
   A. *bad*; since applying discipline for minor violations is a waste of time
   B. *good*; because not applying discipline for minor infractions can lead to a more serious erosion of discipline
   C. *bad*; because employees do not like to be disciplined for minor violations of the rules
   D. *good*; because violating any rule can cause a dangerous situation to occur

22. A maintainer would PROPERLY consider it poor supervisory practice for a foreman to consult with him on
    A. which of several repair jobs should be scheduled first
    B. how to cope with personal problems at home
    C. whether the neatness of his headquarters can be improved
    D. how to express a suggestion which the maintainer plans to submit formally

23. Assume that you have determined that the work of one of your foremen and the men he supervises is consistently behind schedule. When you discuss this situation with the foreman, he tells you that his men are poor workers and then complains that he must spend all of his time checking on their work.
    The following actions are offered for your consideration as possible ways of solving the problem of poor performance of the foreman and his men:
    I. Review the work standards with the foreman and determine whether they are realistic
    II. Tell the foreman that you will recommend him for the foreman's training course for retraining
    III. Ask the foreman for the names of the maintainers and then replace them as soon as possible
    IV. Tell the foreman that you expect him to meet a satisfactory level of performance
    V. Tell the foreman to insist that his men work overtime to catch up to the schedule
    VI. Tell the foreman to review the type and amount of training he has given the maintainers
    VII. Tell the foreman that he will be out of a job if he does not produce on schedule
    VIII. Avoid all criticism of the foreman and his methods

    Which of the following suggested answers CORRECTLY lists the proper actions to be taken to solve the problem of poor performance of the foreman and his men?
    A. I, II, IV, and VI *only*
    B. I, III, V, and VII *only*
    C. II, III, VI, and VIII *only*
    D. IV, V, VI, and VIII *only*

24. When a conference or a group discussion is tending to turn into a *bull session* without constructive purpose, the BEST action to take is to
    A. reprimand the leader of the *bull session*
    B. redirect the discussion to the business at hand
    C. dismiss the meeting and reschedule it for another day
    D. allow the *bull session* to continue

25. Assume that you have been assigned responsibility for a program in which a high production rate is mandatory. From past experience, you know that your foremen do not perform equally well in the various types of jobs given to them.

Which of the following methods should you use in selecting foremen for the specific types of work involved in the program?
  A. Leave the method of selecting foremen to your supervisor
  B. Assign each foreman to the work he does best
  C. Allow each foreman to choose his own job
  D. Assign each foreman to a job which will permit him to improve his own abilities

---

KEY (CORRECT ANSWERS)

1. B	11. C
2. B	12. D
3. A	13. B
4. D	14. B
5. D	15. C
6. B	16. D
7. B	17. C
8. B	18. B
9. A	19. A
10. D	20. B

21. B
22. A
23. A
24. B
25. B

TEST 2

DIRECTIONS: Each question or incomplete statement is followed by several suggested answers or completions. Select the one that BEST answers the question or completes the statement. *PRINT THE LETTER OF THE CORRECT ANSWER IN THE SPACE AT THE RIGHT.*

1. A foreman who is familiar with modern management principles should know that the one of the following requirements of an administrator which is LEAST important is his ability to
    A. coordinate work
    B. plan, organize, and direct the work under his control
    C. cooperate with others
    D. perform the duties of the employees under his jurisdiction

    1.___

2. When subordinates request his advice in solving problems encountered in their work, a certain chief occasionally answers the request by first asking the subordinate what he thinks should be done.
   This action by the chief is, on the whole,
    A. *desirable* because it stimulates subordinates to give more thought to the solution of problems encountered
    B. *undesirable* because it discourages subordinates from asking questions
    C. *desirable* because it discourages subordinates from asking questions
    D. *undesirable* because it undermines the confidence of subordinates in the ability of their supervisor

    2.___

3. Of the following factors that may be considered by a unit head in dealing with the tardy subordinate, the one which should be given LEAST consideration is the
    A. frequency with which the employee is tardy
    B. effect of the employee's tardiness upon the work of other employees
    C. willingness of the employee to work overtime when necessary
    D. cause of the employee's tardiness

    3.___

4. The MOST important requirement of a good inspectional report is that it should be
    A. properly addressed   B. lengthy
    C. clear and brief   D. spelled correctly

    4.___

5. Building superintendents frequently inquire about departmental inspectional procedures.
   Of the following, it is BEST to
    A. advise them to write to the department for an official reply
    B. refuse as the inspectional procedure is a restricted matter
    C. briefly explain the procedure to them
    D. avoid the inquiry by changing the subject

    5.___

6. Reprimanding a crew member before other workers is a
   A. *good practice*; the reprimand serves as a warning to the other workers
   B. *bad practice*; people usually resent criticism made in public
   C. *good practice*; the other workers will realize that the supervisor is fair
   D. *bad practice*; the other workers will take sides in the dispute

7. Of the following actions, the one which is LEAST likely to promote good work is for the group leader to
   A. praise workers for doing a good job
   B. call attention to the opportunities for promotion for better workers
   C. threaten to recommend discharge of workers who are below standard
   D. put into practice any good suggestion made by crew members

8. A supervisor notices that a member of his crew has skipped a routine step in his job.
   Of the following, the BEST action for the supervisor to take is to
   A. promptly question the worker about the incident
   B. immediately assign another man to complete the job
   C. bring up the incident the next time the worker asks for a favor
   D. say nothing about the incident but watch the worker carefully in the future

9. Assume you have been told to show a new worker how to operate a piece of equipment.
   Your FIRST step should be to
   A. ask the worker if he has any questions about the equipment
   B. permit the worker to operate the equipment himself while you carefully watch to prevent damage
   C. demonstrate the operation of the equipment for the worker
   D. have the worker read an instruction booklet on the maintenance of the equipment

10. Whenever a new man was assigned to his crew, the supervisor would introduce him to all other crew members, take him on a tour of the plant, tell him about bus schedules and places to eat.
    This practice is
    A. *good*; the new man is made to feel welcome
    B. *bad*; supervisors should not interfere in personal matters
    C. *good*; the new man knows that he can bring his personal problems to the supervisor
    D. *bad*; work time should not be spent on personal matters

11. The MOST important factor in successful leadership is 11.___
    the ability to
    A. obtain instant obedience to all orders
    B. establish friendly personal relations with crew members
    C. avoid disciplining crew members
    D. make crew members want to do what should be done

12. Explaining the reasons for departmental procedure to 12.___
    workers tends to
    A. waste time which should be used for productive purposes
    B. increase their interest in their work
    C. make them more critical of departmental procedures
    D. confuse them

13. If you want a job done well, do it yourself. 13.___
    For a supervisor to follow this advice would be
    A. *good*; a supervisor is responsible for the work of his crew
    B. *bad*; a supervisor should train his men, not do their work
    C. *good*; a supervisor should be skilled in all jobs assigned to his crew
    D. *bad*; a supervisor loses respect when he works with his hands

14. When a supervisor discovers a mistake in one of the jobs 14.___
    for which his crew is responsible, it is MOST important
    for him to find out
    A. whether anybody else knows about the mistake
    B. who was to blame for the mistake
    C. how to prevent similar mistakes in the future
    D. whether similar mistakes occurred in the past

15. A supervisor who has to explain a new procedure to his 15.___
    crew should realize that questions from the crew USUALLY
    show that they
    A. are opposed to the new procedure
    B. are completely confused by the explanation
    C. need more training in the new procedure
    D. are interested in the explanation

16. A GOOD way for a supervisor to retain the confidence of 16.___
    his or her employees is to
    A. say as little as possible
    B. check work frequently
    C. make no promises unless they will be fulfilled
    D. never hesitate in giving an answer to any question

17. Good supervision is ESSENTIALLY a matter of 17.___
    A. patience in supervising workers
    B. care in selecting workers
    C. skill in human relations
    D. fairness in disciplining workers

18. It is MOST important for an employee who has been assigned 18.____
    a monotonous task to
    A. perform this task before doing other work
    B. ask another employee to help
    C. perform this task only after all other work has been
       completed
    D. take measures to prevent mistakes in performing the
       task

19. One of your employees has violated a minor agency regula- 19.____
    tion.
    The FIRST thing you should do is
    A. warn the employee that you will have to take disci-
       plinary action if it should happen again
    B. ask the employee to explain his or her actions
    C. inform your supervisor and wait for advice
    D. write a memo describing the incident and place it in
       the employee's personnel file

20. One of your employees tells you that he feels you give 20.____
    him much more work than the other employees, and he is
    having trouble meeting your deadlines.
    You should
    A. ask if he has been under a lot of non-work related
       stress lately
    B. review his recent assignments to determine if he is
       correct
    C. explain that this is a busy time, but you are dividing
       the work equally
    D. tell him that he is the most competent employee and
       that is why he receives more work

21. A supervisor assigns one of his crew to complete a portion 21.____
    of a job. A short time later, the supervisor notices that
    the portion has not been completed.
    Of the following, the BEST way for the supervisor to
    handle this is to
    A. ask the crew member why he has not completed the
       assignment
    B. reprimand the crew member for not obeying orders
    C. assign another crew member to complete the assignment
    D. complete the assignment himself

22. Suppose that a member of your crew complains that you are 22.____
    playing favorites in assigning work.
    Of the following, the BEST method of handling the complaint
    is to
    A. deny it and refuse to discuss the matter with the worker
    B. take the opportunity to tell the worker what is wrong
       with his work
    C. ask the worker for examples to prove his point and try
       to clear up any misunderstanding
    D. promise to be more careful in making assignments in
       the future

23. A member of your crew comes to you with a complaint. After discussing the matter with him, it is clear that you have convinced him that his complaint was not justified. At this point, you should
    A. permit him to drop the matter
    B. make him admit his error
    C. pretend to see some justification in his complaint
    D. warn him against making unjustified complaints

24. Suppose that a supervisor has in his crew an older man who works rather slowly. In other respects, this man is a good worker; he is seldom absent, works carefully, never loafs, and is cooperative.
    The BEST way for the supervisor to handle this worker is to
    A. try to get him to work faster and less carefully
    B. give him the most disagreeable job
    C. request that he be given special training
    D. permit him to work at his own speed

25. Suppose that a member of your crew comes to you with a suggestion he thinks will save time in doing a job. You realize immediately that it won't work.
    Under these circumstances, your BEST action would be to
    A. thank the worker for the suggestion and forget about it
    B. explain to the worker why you think it won't work
    C. tell the worker to put the suggestion in writing
    D. ask the other members of your crew to criticize the suggestion

KEY (CORRECT ANSWERS)

1. D	11. D
2. A	12. B
3. C	13. B
4. C	14. C
5. C	15. D
6. B	16. C
7. C	17. C
8. A	18. D
9. C	19. B
10. A	20. B

21. A
22. C
23. A
24. D
25. B

EXAMINATION SECTION

DIRECTIONS FOR THIS SECTION:
Each question or incomplete statement is followed by several suggested answers or completions. Select the one that *BEST* answer the question or completes the statement. *PRINT THE LETTER OF THE CORRECT ANSWER IN THE SPACE AT THE RIGHT.*

TEST 1

1. Although some kinds of instructions are best put in written form, a supervisor can give many instructions verbally. In which one of the following situations would verbal instructions be *MOST* suitable?
    A. Furnishing an employee with the details to be checked in doing a certain job
    B. Instructing an employee on the changes necessary to update the office manual used in your unit
    C. Informing a new employee where different kinds of supplies and equipment that he might need are kept
    D. Presenting an assignment to an employee who will be held accountable for following a series of steps

2. You may be asked to evaluate the organization structure of your unit. Which one of the following questions would you *NOT* expect to take up in an evaluation of this kind?
    A. Is there an employee whose personal problems are interfering with his or her work?
    B. Is there an up-to-date job description for each position in this section?
    C. Are related operations and tasks grouped together and regularly assigned together?
    D. Are responsibilities divided as far as possible, and is this division clearly understood by all employees?

3. In order to distribute and schedule work fairly and efficiently, a supervisor may wish to make a work distribution study. A simple way of getting the information necessary for such a study is to have everyone for one week keep track of each task done and the time spent on each. Which one of the following situations showing up in such a study would *most clearly* call for corrective action?
    A. The newest employee takes longer to do most tasks than do experienced employees
    B. One difficult operation takes longer to do than most other operations carried out by the section
    C. A particular employee is very frequently assigned tasks that are not similar and have no relationship to each other
    D. The most highly skilled employee is often assigned the most difficult jobs

4. The authority to carry out a job can be delegated to a subordinate, but the supervisor remains responsible for the work of the section as a whole. As a supervisor, which of the following rules would be the *BEST* one for you to follow in view of the above statement?
    A. Avoid assigning important tasks to your subordinates, because you will be blamed if anything goes wrong

1. ...

2. ...

3. ...

4. ...

    B. Be sure each subordinate understands the specific job
        he has been assigned, and check at intervals to make
        sure assignments are done properly
    C. Assign several people to every important job, so that
        responsibility will be spread out as much as possible
    D. Have an experienced subordinate check all work done by
        other employees, so that there will be little chance
        of anything going wrong

5. The human tendency to resist change is often reflected in   5. ...
   higher rates of turnover, absenteeism, and errors whenever
   an important change is made in an organization. Although
   psychologists do not fully understand the reasons why people
   resist change, they believe that the resistance stems from a
   threat to the individual's security, that it is a form of fear
   of the unknown.
   In light of this statement, which one of the following approaches would probably be MOST effective in preparing employees for a change in procedure in their unit?
    A. Avoid letting employees know anything about the change
        until the last possible moment
    B. Sympathize with employees who resent the change and
        let them know you share their doubts and fears
    C. Promise the employees that if the change turns out to
        be a poor one, you will allow them to suggest a return
        to the old system
    D. Make sure that employees know the reasons for the change
        and are aware of the benefits that are expected from it

6. Each of the following methods of encouraging employee   6. ...
   participation in work planning has been used effectively
   with different kinds and sizes of employee groups.
   Which one of the following methods would be MOST suitable
   for a group of four technically skilled employees?
    A. Discussions between the supervisor and a representative
        of the group
    B. A suggestion program with semi-annual awards for out-
        standing suggestions
    C. A group discussion summoned whenever a major problem
        remains unsolved for more than a month
    D. Day-to-day exchange of information, opinions and ex-
        perience

7. Of the following, the MOST important reason why a super-   7. ...
   visor is given the authority to tell subordinates what work
   they should do, how they should do it, and when it should
   be done is that *usually*
    A. most people will not work unless there is someone with
        authority standing over them
    B   work is accomplished more effectively if the supervisor
        plans and coordinates it
    C. when division of work is left up to subordinates, there
        is constant arguing, and very little work is accomplished
    D. subordinates are not familiar with the tasks to be
        performed

8. Fatigue is a factor that affects productivity in all work   8. ...
   situations. However, a brief rest period will ordinarily
   serve to restore a person from fatigue.

According to this statement, which one of the following techniques is *most likely* to reduce the impact of fatigue on over-all productivity in a unit?
   A. Scheduling several short breaks throughout the day
   B. Allowing employees to go home early
   C. Extending the lunch period an extra half hour
   D. Rotating job assignments every few weeks

9. After giving a new task to an employee, it is a good idea for a supervisor to ask specific questions to make sure that the employee grasps the essentials of the task and sees how it can be carried out. Questions which ask the employee what he thinks or how he feels about an important aspect of the task are particularly effective.
Which one of the following questions is *NOT* the type of question which would be useful in the foregoing situation?
   A. "Do you feel there will be any trouble meeting the 4:30 deadline?"
   B. "How do you feel about the kind of work we do here?"
   C. "Do you think that combining those two steps will work all right?"
   D. "Can you think of any additional equipment you may need for this process?"

10. Of the following, the *LEAST* important reason for having a *continuous* training program is that
   A. employees may forget procedures that they have already learned
   B. employees may develop short cuts on the job that result in inaccurate work
   C. the job continues to change because of new procedures and equipment
   D. training is one means of measuring effectiveness and productivity on the job

11. In training a new employee, it is usually advisable to break down the job into meaningful parts and have the new employee master one part before going on to the next.
Of the following, the *BEST* reason for using this technique is to
   A. let the new employee know the reason for what he is doing and thus encourage him to remain in the unit
   B. make the employee aware of the importance of the work and encourage him to work harder
   C. show the employee that the work is easy so that he will be encouraged to work faster
   D. make it more likely that the employee will experience success and will be encouraged to continue learning the job

12. You may occasionally find a serious error in the work of one of your subordinates.
Of the following, the *BEST* time to discuss such an error with an employee *usually* is
   A. immediately after the error is found
   B. after about two weeks, since you will also be able to point out some good things that the employee has accomplished

    C. when you have discovered a pattern of errors on the part of this employee so that he will not be able to dispute your criticism
    D. after the error results in a complaint by your own supervisor

13. For very important announcements to the staff, a supervisor should usually use both written and oral communications. For example, when a new procedure is to be introduced, the supervisor can more easily obtain the group's acceptance by giving his subordinates a rough draft of the new procedure and calling a meeting of all his subordinates. The *LEAST* important benefit of this technique is that it will better enable the supervisor to
    A. explain why the change is necessary
    B. make adjustments in the new procedure to meet valid staff objections
    C. assign someone to carry out the new procedure
    D. answer questions about the new procedure

14. Assume that, while you are interviewing an individual to obtain information, the individual pauses in the middle of an answer.
The *BEST* of the following actions for you to take at that time is to
    A. correct any inaccuracies in what he has said
    B. remain silent until he continues
    C. explain your position on the matter being discussed
    D. explain that time is short and that he must complete his story quickly

15. When you are interviewing someone to obtain information, the *BEST* of the following reasons for you to repeat certain of his exact words is to
    A. assure him that appropriate action will be taken
    B. encourage him to switch to another topic of discussion
    C. assure him that you agree with his point of view
    D. encourage him to elaborate on a point he has made

16. Generally, when writing a letter, the use of precise words and concise sentences is
    A. *good*, because less time will be required to write the letter
    B. *bad*, because it is most likely that the reader will think the letter is unimportant and will not respond favorably
    C. *good*, because it is likely that your desired meaning will be conveyed to the reader
    D. *bad*, because your letter will be too brief to provide adequate information

17. In which of the following cases would it be *MOST* desirable to have *two* cards for one individual in a *single* alphabetic file? The individual has
    A. a hyphenated surname   B. two middle names
    C. a first name with an unusual spelling
    D. a compound first name

18. Of the following, it is *MOST* appropriate to use a form letter when it is necessary to answer many
    A. requests or inquiries from a single individual

    B. follow-up letters from individuals requesting additional information
    C. requests or inquiries about a single subject
    D. complaints from individuals that they have been unable to obtain various types of information

19. Assume that you are asked to make up a budget for your section for the coming year, and you are told that the most important function of the budget is its "control function."
Of the following, "control" in this context implies, *most nearly*, that
    A. you will probably be asked to justify expenditures in any category when it looks as though these expenditures are departing greatly from the amount budgeted
    B. your section will probably not be allowed to spend more than the budgeted amount in any given category, although it is always permissible to spend less
    C. your section will be required to spend the exact amount budgeted in every category
    D. the budget will be filed in the Office of the Comptroller so that when the year is over the actual expenditures can be compared with the amounts in the budget

20. In writing a report, the practice of taking up the *least* important points *first* and the *most* important points *last* is a
    A. *good technique* since the final points made in a report will make the greatest impression on the reader
    B. *good technique* since the material is presented in a more logical manner and will lead directly to the conclusions
    C. *poor technique* since the reader's time is wasted by having to review irrelevant information before finishing the report
    D. *poor technique* since it may cause the reader to lose interest in the report and arrive at incorrect conclusions about the report

21. Typically, when the technique of "supervision by results" is practiced, higher management sets down, either implicitly or explicitly, certain performance standards or goals that the subordinate is expected to meet. So long as these standards are met, management interferes very little.
The *most likely* result of the use of this technique is that it will
    A. lead to ambiguity in terms of goals
    B. be successful only to the extent that close direct supervision is practiced
    C. make it possible to evaluate both employee and supervisory effectiveness
    D. allow for complete dependence on the subordinate's part

22. When making written evaluations and reviews of the performance of subordinates, it is *usually ADVISABLE* to
    A. avoid informing the employee of the evaluation if it is critical because it may create hard feelings
    B. avoid informing the employee of the evaluation whether critical or favorable because it is tension-producing

C. to permit the employee to see the evaluation but not to discuss it with him because the supervisor cannot be certain where the discussion might lead
D. to discuss the evaluation openly with the employee because it helps the employee understand what is expected of him

23. There are a number of well-known and respected human relations principles that successful supervisors have been using for years in building good relationships with their employees. Which of the following does *NOT* illustrate such a principle?
    A. Give clear and complete instructions
    B. Let each person know how he is getting along
    C. Keep an open-door policy
    D. Make all relationships personal ones

24. Assume that it is necessary for you to give an unpleasant assignment to one of your subordinates. You expect this employee to raise some objections to this assignment.
The *most appropriate* of the following actions for you to take *FIRST* is to issue the assignment
    A. *orally*, with the further statement that you will not listen to any complaints
    B. *in writing*, to forestall any complaints by the employee
    C. *orally*, permitting the employee to express his feelings
    D. *in writing*, with a note that any comments should be submitted in writing

25. Suppose you have just announced at a staff meeting with your subordinates that a radical reorganization of work will take place next week. Your subordinates at the meeting appear to be excited, tense, and worried.
Of the following, the *BEST* action for you to take at that time is to
    A. schedule private conferences with each subordinate to obtain his reaction to the meeting
    B. close the meeting and tell your subordinates to return immediately to their work assignments
    C. give your subordinates some time to ask questions and discuss your announcement
    D. insist that your subordinates do not discuss your announcement among themselves or with other members of the agency

TEST 2

1. Of the following, the *BEST* way for a supervisor to increase employees' interest in their work is to
    A. allow them to make as many decisions as possible
    B. demonstrate to them that he is as technically competent as they
    C. give each employee a difficult assignment
    D. promptly convey to them instructions from higher management

2. The *one* of the following which is *LEAST* important in maintaining a high level of productivity on the part of employees is the

    A. provision of optimum physical working conditions for employees
    B. strength of employees' aspirations for promotion
    C. anticipated satisfactions which employees hope to derive from their work
    D. employees' interest in their jobs

3. Of the following, the *MAJOR* advantage of group problem-solving, as compared to individual problem-solving, is that groups will *more readily*
    A. abide by their own decisions
    B. agree with agency management
    C. devise new policies and procedures
    D. reach conclusions sooner

4. The group problem-solving conference is a useful supervisory method for getting people to reach solutions to problems.
Of the following the *reason* that groups usually reach more realistic solutions than do individuals is that
    A. individuals, as a rule, take longer than do groups in reaching decisions and are therefore more likely to make an error
    B. bringing people together to let them confer impresses participants with the seriousness of problems
    C. groups are generally more concerned with the future in evaluating organizational problems
    D. the erroneous opinions of group members tend to be corrected by the other members

5. A competent supervisor should be able to distinguish between human and technical problems.
Of the following, the *MAJOR* difference between such problems is that serious human problems, in comparison to ordinary technical problems,
    A. are remedied more quickly
    B. involve a lesser need for diagnosis
    C. are more difficult to define
    D. become known through indications which are usually the actual problem

6. Of the following, the *BEST* justification for a public agency establishing an alcoholism program for its employees is that
    A. alcoholism has traditionally been looked upon with a certain amused tolerance by management and thereby ignored as a serious illness
    B. employees with drinking problems have twice as many on-the-job accidents, especially during the early years of the problem
    C. excessive use of alcohol is associated with personality instability hindering informal social relationships among peers and subordinates
    D. the agency's public reputation will suffer despite an employee's drinking problem being a personal matter of little public concern

7. Assume you are a manager and you find a group of maintenance employees assigned to your project drinking and playing cards for money in an incinerator room after their regular working hours.

The one of the following actions it would be BEST for you to take is to
- A. suspend all employees immediately if there is no question in your mind as to the validity of the charges
- B. review the personnel records of those involved with the supervisor and make a joint decision on which employees should sustain penalties of loss of annual leave or fines
- C. ask the supervisor to interview each violator and submit written reports to you and thereafter consult with the supervisor about disciplinary actions
- D. deduct three days of annual leave from each employee involved if he pleads guilty in lieu of facing more serious charges

8. Assume that as a manager you must discipline a subordinate, but all of the pertinent facts necessary for a full determination of the appropriate disciplinary action to take are not yet available. However, you fear that a delay in disciplinary action may damage the morale of other employees.
The one of the following which is MOST appropriate for you to do in this matter is to
- A. take immediate disciplinary action as if all the pertinent facts were available
- B. wait until all the pertinent facts are available before reaching a decision
- C. inform the subordinate that you know he is guilty, issue a stern warning, and then let him wait for your further action
- D. reduce the severity of the discipline appropriate for the violation

8. ...

9. There are two standard dismissal procedures utilized by most public agencies. The first is the "open back door" policy, in which the decision of a supervisor in discharging an employee for reasons of inefficiency cannot be cancelled by the central personnel agency. The second is the "closed back door" policy, in which the central personnel agency can order the supervisor to restore the discharged employee to his position.
Of the following, the major DISADVANTAGE of the "closed back door" policy as opposed to the "open back door" policy is that central personnel agencies are
- A. likely to approve the dismissal of employees when there is inadequate justification
- B. likely to revoke dismissal actions out of sympathy for employees
- C. less qualified than employing agencies to evaluate the efficiency of employees
- D. easily influenced by political, religious, and racial factors

9. ...

10. The one of the following for which a formal grievance-handling system is LEAST useful is in
- A. reducing the frequency of employee complaints
- B. diminishing the likelihood of arbitrary action by supervisors
- C. providing an outlet for employee frustrations

10. ...

      D. bringing employee problems to the attention of higher management
11. The one of the following managers whose leadership style involves the *GREATEST* delegation of authority to subordinates is the one who presents to subordinates
      A. his ideas and invites questions
      B. his decision and persuades them to accept it
      C. the problem, gets their suggestions, and makes his decision
      D. a tentative decision which is subject to change
12. Which of the following is *most likely* to cause employee productivity standards to be set too high?
      A. Standards of productivity are set by first-line supervisors rather than by higher-level managers.
      B. Employees' opinions about productivity standards are sought through written questionnaires.
      C. Initial studies concerning productivity are conducted by staff specialists.
      D. Ideal work conditions assumed in the productivity standards are lacking in actual operations.
13. The one of the following which states the *MAIN* value of an organization chart for a manager is that such charts show the
      A. lines of formal authority
      B. manner in which duties are performed by each employee
      C. flow of work among employees on the same level
      D. specific responsibilities of each position
14. Which of the following *BEST* names the usual role of a line unit with regard to the organization's programs?
      A. Seeking publicity   B. Developing
      C. Carrying out   D. Evaluating
15. Critics of promotion *from within* a public agency argue for hiring *from outside* the agency because they believe that promotion from within leads to
      A. resentment and consequent weakened morale on the part of those not promoted
      B. the perpetuation of outdated practices and policies
      C. a more complex hiring procedure than hiring from outside the agency
      D. problems of objectively appraising someone already in the organization
16. The one of the following management functions which *usually* can be handled *MOST* effectively by a committee is the
      A. settlement of interdepartmental disputes
      B. planning of routine work schedules
      C. dissemination of information
      D. assignment of personnel
17. Assume that you are serving on a committee which is considering proposals in order to recommend a new maintenance policy. After eliminating a number of proposals by unanimous consent, the committee is deadlocked on three proposals.
The one of the following which is the *BEST* way for the committee to reach agreement on a proposal they could recommend is to
      A. consider and vote on each proposal separately by secret ballot

    B. examine and discuss the three proposals until the proponents of two of them are persuaded they are wrong
    C. reach a synthesis which incorporates the significant features of each proposal
    D. discuss the three proposals until the proponents of each one concede those aspects of the proposals about which there is disagreement

18. A commonly used training and development method for professional staff is the case method, which utilizes the description of a situation, real or simulated, to provide a common base for analysis, discussion, and problem-solving.
Of the following, the MOST appropriate time to use the case method is when professional staff needs
    A. insight into their personality problems
    B. practice in applying management concepts to their own problems
    C. practical experience in the assignment of delegated responsibilities
    D. to know how to function in many different capacities

19. The incident process is a training and development method in which trainees are given a very brief statement of an event or of a situation presenting a job incident or an employee problem of special significance.
Of the following, it is MOST appropriate to use the incident process when
    A. trainees need to learn to review and analyze facts before solving a problem
    B. there are a large number of trainees who require the same information
    C. there are too many trainees to carry on effective discussion
    D. trainees are not aware of the effect of their behavior on others

20. The one of the following types of information about which a new clerical employee is usually LEAST concerned during the orientation process is
    A. his specific job duties   B. where he will work
    C. his organization's history D. who his associates will be

21. The one of the following which is the MOST important limitation on the degree to which work should be broken down into specialized tasks is the point at which
    A. there ceases to be sufficient work of a specialized nature to occupy employees
    B. training costs equal the half-yearly savings derived from further specialization
    C. supervision of employees performing specialized tasks becomes more technical than supervision of general employees
    D. it becomes more difficult to replace the specialist than to replace the generalist who performs a complex set of functions

22. When a supervisor is asked for his opinion of the suitability for promotion of a subordinate, the supervisor is actually being asked to predict the subordinate's future behavior in a new role.

Such a prediction is *most likely* to be accurate if the
- A. higher position is similar to the subordinate's current one
- B. higher position requires intangible personal qualities
- C. new position requires a high intellectual level of performance
- D. supervisor has had little personal association with the subordinate away from the job

23. In one form of the non-directive evaluation interview the supervisor communicates his evaluation to the employee and then listens to the employee's response without making further suggestions.
The one of the following which is the PRINCIPAL danger of this method of evaluation is that the employee is most likely to
    - A. develop an indifferent attitude towards the supervisor
    - B. fail to discover ways of improving his performance
    - C. become resistant to change in the organization's structure
    - D. place the blame for his shortcomings on his co-workers

24. In establishing rules for his subordinates, a superior should be PRIMARILY concerned with
    - A. creating sufficient flexibility to allow for exceptions
    - B. making employees aware of the reasons for the rules and the penalties for infractions
    - C. establishing the strength of his own position in relation to his subordinates
    - D. having his subordinates know that such rules will be imposed in a personal manner

25. The practice of conducting staff training sessions on a periodic basis is *generally* considered
    - A. *poor;* it takes employees away from their work assignments
    - B. *poor;* all staff training should be done on an individual basis
    - C. *good;* it permits the regular introduction of new methods and techniques
    - D. *good;* it ensures a high employee productivity rate

KEYS (CORRECT ANSWERS)

TEST 1

1.	C	6.	D	11.	D	16.	C	21.	C
2.	A	7.	B	12.	A	17.	A	22.	D
3.	C	8.	A	13.	C	18.	C	23.	D
4.	B	9.	B	14.	B	19.	A	24.	C
5.	D	10.	D	15.	D	20.	D	25.	C

TEST 2

1.	A	6.	B	11.	C	16.	A	21.	A
2.	A	7.	C	12.	D	17.	C	22.	A
3.	A	8.	B	13.	A	18.	B	23.	B
4.	D	9.	C	14.	C	19.	A	24.	B
5.	C	10.	A	15.	B	20.	C	25.	C

EXAMINATION SECTION

TEST 1

DIRECTIONS: Each question or incomplete statement is followed by several suggested answers or completions. Select the one that BEST answers the question or completes the statement. *PRINT THE LETTER OF THE CORRECT ANSWER IN THE SPACE AT THE RIGHT.*

1. Following are three statements concerning on-the-job training:
    I. On-the-job training is rarely used as a method of training employees.
    II. On-the-job training is often carried on with little or no planning.
    III. On-the-job training is often less expensive than other types.

    Which of the following BEST classifies the above statements into those that are correct and those that are not?
    A. I is correct, but II and III are not
    B. II is correct, but I and III are not
    C. I and II are correct, but III is not
    D. II and III are correct, but I is not

1.____

2. The one of the following which is NOT a valid principle for a supervisor to keep in mind when talking to a subordinate about his performance is:
    A. People frequently know when they deserve criticism
    B. Supervisors should be prepared to offer suggestions to subordinates about how to improve their work
    C. Good points should be discussed before bad points
    D. Magnifying a subordinate's faults will get him to improve faster

2.____

3. In many organizations information travels quickly through the "grapevine".
    Following are three statements concerning the "grapevine":
    I. Information a subordinate does not want to tell her supervisor may reach the supervisor through the "grapevine".
    II. A supervisor can often do her job better by knowing the information that travels through the "grapevine".
    III. A supervisor can depend on the "grapevine" as a way to get accurate information from the employees on his staff

    Which one of the following *correctly* classifies the above statements into those which are generally CORRECT and those which are NOT?
    A. II is correct, but I and III are not
    B. III is correct, but I and II are not
    C. I and II are correct, but III is not
    D. I and III are correct, but II is not

3.____

4. Following are three statements concerning supervision:
   I. A supervisor knows he is doing a good job if his subordinates depend upon him to make every decision.
   II. A supervisor who delegates authority to his subordinates soon finds that his subordinates begin to resent him.
   III. Giving credit for good work is frequently an effective method of getting subordinates to work harder.

   Which one of the following *correctly* classifies the above statements into those that are CORRECT and those that are NOT?
   A. I and II are correct, but III is not
   B. II and III are correct, but I is not
   C. II is correct, but I and III are not
   D. III is correct, but I and II are not

5. Of the following, the LEAST appropriate action for a supervisor to take in preparing a disciplinary case against a subordinate is to
   A. keep careful records of each incident in which the subordinate has been guilty of misconduct or incompetency, even though immediate disciplinary action may not be necessary
   B. discuss with the employee each incident of misconduct as it occurs so the employee knows where he stands
   C. accept memoranda from any other employees who may have been witnesses to acts of misconduct
   D. keep the subordinate's personnel file confidential so that he is unaware of the evidence being gathered against him

6. Praise by a supervisor can be an important element in motivating subordinates.
   Following are three statements concerning a supervisor's praise of subordinates:
   I. In order to be effective, praise must be lavish and constantly restated.
   II. Praise should be given in a manner which meets the needs of the individual subordinate.
   III. The subordinate whose work is praised should believe that the praise is earned.

   Which of the following *correctly* classifies the above statements into those that are CORRECT and those that are NOT?
   A. I is correct, but II and III are not
   B. II and III are correct, but I is not
   C. III is correct, but I and II are not
   D. I and II are correct, but III is not

7. A supervisor feels that he is about to lose his temper while reprimanding a subordinate.
   Of the following, the BEST action for the supervisor to take is to
   A. postpone the reprimand for a short time until his self-control is assured
   B. continue the reprimand because a loss of temper by the supervisor will show the subordinate the seriousness of the error he made

C. continue the reprimand because failure to do so will show that the supervisor does not have complete self-control
D. postpone the reprimand until the subordinate is capable of understanding the reason for the supervisor's loss of temper

8. Following are three statements concerning various ways of giving orders to subordinates:
   I. An implied order or suggestion is usually appropriate for the inexperienced employee.
   II. A polite request is less likely to upset a sensitive subordinate than a direct order.
   III. A direct order is usually appropriate in an emergency situation.

   Which of the following *correctly* classifies the above statements into those that are CORRECT and those that are NOT?
   A. I is correct, but II and III are not
   B. II and III are correct, but I is not
   C. III is correct, but I and II are not
   D. I and II are correct, but III is not

8.____

9. The one of the following which is NOT an acceptable reason for taking disciplinary action against a subordinate guilty of serious violations of the rules is that
   A. the supervisor can "let off steam" against subordinates who break rules frequently
   B. a subordinate whose work continues to be unsatisfactory may be terminated
   C. a subordinate may be encouraged to improve his work
   D. an example is set for other employees

9.____

10. At the first meeting with your staff after appointment as a supervisor, you find considerable indifference and some hostility among the participants.
    Of the following, the *most appropriate* way to handle this situation is to
    A. disregard the attitudes displayed and continue to make your presentation until you have completed it
    B. discontinue your presentation but continue the meeting and attempt to find out the reasons for their attitudes
    C. warm up your audience with some good natured statements and anecdotes and then proceed with your presentation
    D. discontinue the meeting and set up personal interviews with the staff members to try to find out the reason for their attitude

10.____

11. Use a written rather than oral communication to amend any previous written communication.
    Of the following, the BEST justification for this statement is that
    A. oral changes will be considered more impersonal and thus less important
    B. oral changes will be forgotten or recalled indifferently
    C. written communications are clearer and shorter
    D. written communications are better able to convey feeling tone

11.____

12. Assume that a certain supervisor, when writing important communications to his subordinates, often repeats certain points in different words.
    This technique is *generally*
    A. *ineffective*; it tends to confuse rather than help
    B. *effective*; it tends to improve understanding by the subordinates
    C. *ineffective*; it unnecessarily increases the length of the communication and may annoy the subordinates
    D. *effective*; repetition is always an advantage in communications

13. In preparing a letter or a report, a supervisor may wish to persuade the reader of the correctness of some idea or course of action.
    The BEST way to accomplish this is for the supervisor to
    A. encourage the reader to make a prompt decision
    B. express each idea in a separate paragraph
    C. present the subject matter of the letter in the first paragraph
    D. state the potential benefits for the reader

14. Effective communications, a basic necessity for successful supervision is a two-way street. A good supervisor needs to listen to, as well as disseminate, information and he must be able to encourage his subordinates to communicate with him.
    Which of the following suggestions will contribute LEAST to improving the "listening power" of a supervisor?
    A. Don't assume anything; don't anticipate, and don't let a subordinate think you know what he is going to say
    B. Don't interupt; let him have his full say even if it requires a second session that day to get the full story
    C. React quickly to his statements so that he knows you are interested, even if you must draw some conclusions prematurely
    D. Try to understand the real need for his talking to you even if it is quite different from the subject under discussion

15. Of the following, the MOST useful approach for the supervisor to take toward the informal employee communications network know as the "grapevine" is to
    A. remain isolated from it, but not take any active steps to eliminate it
    B. listen to it, but not depend on it for accurate information
    C. use it to disseminate confidential information
    D. eliminate it as diplomatically as possible

16. If a supervisor is asked to estimate the number of employees that he believes he will need in his unit in the coming fiscal year, the supervisor should FIRST attempt to learn the
    A. nature and size of the workload his unit will have during that time
    B. cost of hiring and training new employees
    C. average number of employee absences per year
    D. number of employees needed to indirectly support or assist his unit

17. An important supervisory responsibility is coordinating the operations of the unit. This may include setting work schedules, controlling work quality, establishing interim due dates, etc. In order to handle this task it has been divided into the following five stages:
    I. Determine the steps or sequence required for the tasks to be performed.
    II. Give the orders, either written or oral, to begin work on the tasks.
    III. Check up by following each task to make sure it is proceeding according to plan.
    IV. Schedule the jobs by setting a time for each task of operation to begin and end.
    V. Control the process by correcting conditions which interfere with the plan.

    The MOST logical sequence in which these planning steps should be performed is
    A. I, II, III, IV, V
    B. II, I, V, III, IV
    C. I, IV, II, III, V
    D. IV, I, II, III, V

18. Assume that a supervisor calls a meeting with the staff under his supervision in order to discuss several proposals. After some discussion, he realizes that he strongly disagrees with one proposal that four of the staff have rather firmly favored.
    At this point, he could BEST handle the situation by saying
    A. "I have the responsibility for this decision, and I must disagree."
    B. "I am just reminding you that I have had a great deal more experience in these matters."
    C. "You have presented some good points, but perhaps we could look at it another way."
    D. "The only way that this proposal can be disposed of is to defer it for further discussion."

19. As far as the social activities and groups of his subordinates are concerned, a supervisor in a large organization can BEST strengthen his tools of leadership by
    A. emphasizing the organization as a whole and forbidding the formation of groups
    B. ignoring the groups as much as possible and dealing with each subordinate as an individual
    C. learning about the status structure of employee groups and their values
    D. avoiding any relationship with groups

20. If a subordinate asks you, his supervisor, for advice in planning his career in the department you *should*
    A. encourage him to feel that he can easily reach the top of his occupational ladder
    B. discourage him from setting his hopes too high
    C. discuss career opportunities realistically with him
    D. explain that you have no control over his opportunities for advancement

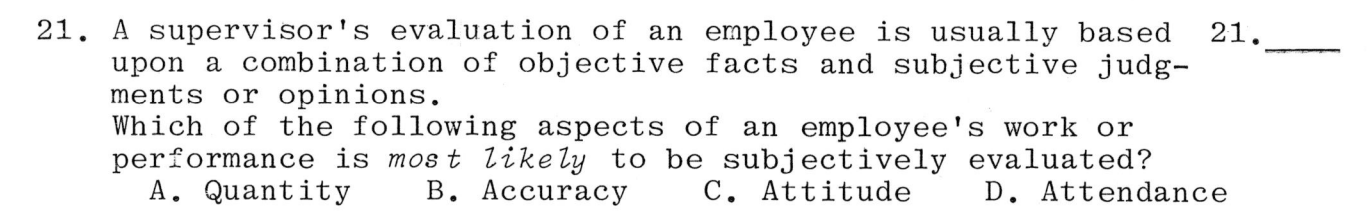

21. A supervisor's evaluation of an employee is usually based upon a combination of objective facts and subjective judgments or opinions.
    Which of the following aspects of an employee's work or performance is *most likely* to be subjectively evaluated?
       A. Quantity   B. Accuracy   C. Attitude   D. Attendance

22. Of the following possible characteristics of supervisors, the one *most likely* to lead to failure as a supervisor is
    A. a tendency to seek several opinions before making decisions in complex matters
    B. lack of a strong desire to advance to a top position in management
    C. little formal training in human relations skills
    D. poor relations with subordinates and other supervisory personnel

23. People who break rules do so for a number of reasons. However, employees will break rules *less* often if
    A. the supervisor uses his own judgment about work methods
    B. the supervisor pretends to act strictly, but isn't really serious about it
    C. they greatly enjoy their work
    D. they have completed many years of service

24. Assume that an employee under your supervision has become resentful and generally noncooperative after his request for transfer to another office closer to his place of residence was denied. The request was denied primarily because of the importance of his current assignment. The employee has been a valued worker, but you are now worried that his resentful attitude will have a detrimental effect.
    Of the following, the MOST desirable way for you to handle this situation is to
    A. arrange for the employee;s transfer to the office he originally requested
    B. arrange for the employee's transfer to another office, but not the one he originally requested
    C. attempt to re-focus the employee's attention on those aspects of his current assignment which will be most rewarding and satisfying to him
    D. explain to the employee that, while you are sympathetic to his request, department rules will not allow transfers for reasons of personal convenience

25. Of the following, it would be LEAST advisable for a supervisor to use his administrative authority to affect the behavior and activities of his subordinates when he is trying to
    A. change the way his subordinates perform a particular task
    B. establish a minimum level of conformity to established rules
    C. bring about change in the attitudes of his subordinates
    D. improve the speed with which his subordinates respond to his orders

26. Assume that a supervisor gives his subordinate instructions which are appropriate and clear. The subordinate thereupon refuses to follow these instructions.
Of the following, it would then be MOST appropriate for the supervisor to
   A. attempt to find out what it is that the employee objects to
   B. take disciplinary action that same day
   C. remind the subordinate about supervisory authority and threaten him with discipline
   D. insist that the subordinate carry out the order immediately

27. Of the following, the MOST effective way to identify training needs resulting from gradual changes in procedure is to
   A. monitor on a continuous basis the actual jobs performed and the skills required
   B. periodically send out a written questionnaire asking personnel to identify their needs
   C. conduct interviews at regular intervals with selected employees
   D. consult employees' personnel records

28. Assume that you, as a supervisor, have had a new employee assigned to you. If the duties of his position can be broken into independent parts, which of the following is usually the BEST way to train this new employee?
Start with
   A. the easiest duties and progressively proceed to the most difficult
   B. something easy; move to something difficult; then back to something easy
   C. something difficult; move to something easy; then to something difficult
   D. the most difficult duties and progressively proceed to the easiest

29. The oldest and most commonly used training technique is on-the-job training. Instruction is given to the worker by his supervisor or by another employee. Such training is essential in most jobs, although it is not always effective when used alone.
This technique, however, *can* be effectively used alone if
   A. the skills involved can be learned quickly
   B. a large number of people are to be trained at one time
   C. other forms of training have not been previously used with the people involved
   D. the skills to be taught are mental rather than manual

30. It is generally agreed that the learning process is facilitated in proportion to the amount of feedback that the learner is given about his performance.
Following are three statements concerning the learning process:
   I. The more specific the learner's knowledge of how he performed, the more rapid his improvement and the higher his level of performance.
   II. Giving the learner knowledge of his results does not affect his motivation to learn.

III. Learners who are not given feedback will set up subjective criteria and evaluate their own performance.

Which of the following choices lists ALL of the above statements that are *generally* correct?
   A. I and II *only*
   C. II and III *only*
   B. I and III *only*
   D. I, II and III

KEY (CORRECT ANSWERS)

1. D	11. B	21. C
2. D	12. B	22. D
3. C	13. D	23. C
4. D	14. C	24. C
5. D	15. B	25. C
6. B	16. A	26. A
7. A	17. C	27. A
8. B	18. C	28. A
9. A	19. C	29. A
10. D	20. C	30. B

TEST 2

DIRECTIONS: Each question or incomplete statement is followed by several suggested answers or completions. Select the one that BEST answers the question or completes the statement. *PRINT THE LETTER OF THE CORRECT ANSWER IN THE SPACE AT THE RIGHT.*

Questions 1-6.

DIRECTIONS: Questions 1 through 6 are to be answered SOLELY on the basis of the information given in the following paragraph.

    The use of role-playing as a training technique was developed during the past decade by social scientists, particularly psychologists, who have been active in training experiments. Originally, this technique was applied by clinical psychologists who discovered that a patient appears to gain understanding of an emotionally disturbing situation when encouraged to act out roles in that situation. As applied in government and business organizations, the purpose of role-playing is to aid employees to understand certain work problems involving interpersonal relations and to enable observers to evaluate various reactions to them. Thus, for example, on the problem of handling grievances, two individuals from the group might be selected to act out extemporaneously the parts of subordinate and supervisor. When this situation is enacted by various pairs among the class and the techniques and results are discussed, the members of the group are presumed to reach conclusions about the most effective means of handling similar situations. Often the use of role reversal, where participants take parts different from their actual work roles, assists individuals to gain more insight into other people's problems and viewpoints. Although role-playing can be a rewarding training device, the trainer must be aware of his responsibilities. If this technique is to be successful, thorough briefing of both actors and observers as to the situation in question, the participants' roles, and what to look for, is essential.

1. The role-playing technique was FIRST used for the purpose of
   A. measuring the effectiveness of training programs
   B. training supervisors in business organizations
   C. treating emotionally disturbed patients
   D. handling employee grievances

1.___

2. When role-playing is used in private business as a training device, the CHIEF aim is to
   A. develop better relations between supervisor and subordinate in the handling of grievances
   B. come up with a solution to a specific problem that has arisen
   C. determine the training needs of the group
   D. increase employee understanding of the human relation factors in work situations

2.___

3. From the above passage, it is MOST reasonable to conclude that when role-playing is used, it is preferable to have the roles acted out by
   A. only one set of actors
   B. no more than two sets of actors
   C. several different sets of actors
   D. the trainer or trainers of the group

3.___

4. Based on the above passage, a trainer using the technique of role reversal in a problem of first-line supervision should assign a senior employee to play the part of a(n)
   A. new employee   B. senior employee
   C. principal employee   D. angry citizen

4.___

5. It can be inferred from the above passage that a limitation of role-play as a training method is that
   A. many work situations do not lend themselves to role-play
   B. employees are not experienced enough as actors to play the roles realistically
   C. only trainers who have psychological training can use it successfully
   D. participants who are observing and not acting do not benefit from it

5.___

6. To obtain good results from the use of role-play in training, a trainer should give participants
   A. a minimum of information about the situation so that they can act spontaneously
   B. scripts which illustrate the best method for handling the situation
   C. a complete explanation of the problem and the roles to be acted out
   D. a summary of work problems which involve interpersonal relations

6.___

7. Of the following, the MOST important reason for a supervisor to prepare good written reports is that
   A. a supervisor is rated on the quality of his reports
   B. decisions are often made on the basis of the reports
   C. such reports take less time for superiors to review
   D. such reports demonstrate efficiency of department operations

7.___

8. Of the following, the BEST test of a good report is whether it
   A. provides the information needed
   B. shows the good sense of the writer
   C. is prepared according to a proper format
   D. is grammatical and neat

8.___

9. When a supervisor writes a report, he can BEST show that   9.___
   he has an understanding of the subject of the report by
      A. including necessary facts and omitting non-essential
         details
      B. using statistical data
      C. giving his conclusions but not the data on which
         they are based
      D. using a technical vocabulary

10. Suppose you and another supervisor on the same level are   10.___
    assigned to work together on a report. You disagree
    strongly with one of the recommendations the other super-
    visor wants to include in the report but you cannot
    change his views.
    Of the following, it would be BEST that
       A. you refuse to accept responsibility for the report
       B. you ask that someone else be assigned to this project
          to replace you
       C. each of you state his own ideas about this recom-
          mendation in the report
       D. you give in to the other supervisor's opinion for
          the sake of harmony

11. Standardized forms are often provided for submitting   11.___
    reports.
    Of the following, the MOST important advantage of using
    standardized forms for reports is that
       A. they take less time to prepare than individually
          written reports
       B. necessary information is less likely to be omitted
       C. the responsibility for preparing these reports can
          be delegated to subordinates
       D. the person making the report can omit information
          he considers unimportant

12. A report which may BEST be classed as a *periodic* report 12.___
    is one which
       A. requires the same type of information at regular
          intervals
       B. contains detailed information which is to be retained
          in permanent records
       C. is prepared whenever a special situation occurs
       D. lists information in graphic form

13. Which one of the following is NOT an important reason   13.___
    for keeping accurate records in an office?
       A. Facts will be on hand when decisions have to be made.
       B. The basis for past actions can be determined.
       C. Information needed by other bureaus can be furnished.
       D. Filing is easier when records are properly made out.

14. Suppose you are preparing to write a report recommending   14.___
    a change in a certain procedure. You learn that another
    supervisor made a report a few years ago suggesting a
    change in this same procedure, but that no action was
    taken.

Of the following, it would be MOST desirable for you to
- A. avoid reading the other supervisor's report so that you will write with a more up-to-date point of view
- B. make no recommendation since management seems to be against any change in the procedure
- C. read the other report before you write your report to see what bearing it may have on your recommendations
- D. avoid including in your report any information that can be obtained by referring to the other report

15. If a report you are preparing to your superior is going to be a very long one, it would be DESIRABLE to include a summary of your basic conclusions
    - A. at the end of the report
    - B. at the beginning of the report
    - C. in a separate memorandum
    - D. right after you present the supporting data

16. Suppose that some bureau and department policies must be very frequently applied by your subordinates while others rarely come into use.
    As a supervising employee, a GOOD technique for you to use in fulfilling your responsibility of seeing to it that policies are adhered to is to
    - A. ask the director of the bureau to issue to all employees an explanation in writing of all policies
    - B. review with your subordinates every week those policies which have daily application
    - C. follow up on and explain at regular intervals the application of those policies which are not used very often by your subordinates
    - D. recommend to your superiors that policies rarely used be changed or dropped

17. The BASIC purpose behind the principle of delegation of authority is to
    - A. give the supervisor who is delegating a chance to acquire skills in higher level functions
    - B. free the supervisor from routine tasks in order that he may do the important parts of his job
    - C. prevent supervisors from overstepping the lines of authority which have been established
    - D. place the work delegated in the hands of those employees who can perform it best

18. A district commander can BEST assist management in long-range planning by
    - A. reporting to his superiors any changing conditions in the district
    - B. maintaining a neat and efficiently run office
    - C. scheduling work so that areas with a high rate of non-compliance get more intensive coverage
    - D. properly training new personnel assigned to his district

19. Suppose that new quarters have been rented for your district office.
Of the following, the LEAST important factor to be considered in planning the layout of the office is the
   A. need for screening confidential activities from unauthorized persons
   B. relative importance of the various types of work
   C. areas of noise concentration
   D. convenience with which communication between sections of the office can be achieved

20. Of the following, the MOST basic effect of organizing a department so that lines of authority are clearly defined and duties are specifically assigned is to
   A. increase the need for close supervision
   B. decrease the initiative of subordinates
   C. lessen the possibility of duplication of work
   D. increase the responsibilities of supervisory personnel

21. An accepted management principle is that decisions should be delegated to the lowest point in the organization at which they can be made effectively.
The one of the following which is MOST likely to be a result of the application of this principle is that
   A. no factors will be overlooked in making decisions
   B. prompt action will follow the making of decisions
   C. decisions will be made more rapidly
   D. coordination of decisions that are made will be simplified

22. Suppose you are a supervisor and need some guidance from a higher authority.
In which one of the following situations would it be PERMISSIBLE for you to bypass the regular upward channels of communication in the chain of command?
   A. In an emergency when your superior is not available
   B. When it is not essential to get a quick reply
   C. When you feel your immediate superior is not understanding of the situation
   D. When you want to obtain information that you think your superior does not have

23. Of the following, the CHIEF limitation of the organization chart as it is generally used in business and government is that the chart
   A. makes lines of responsibility and authority undesirably definite and formal
   B. is often out of date as soon as it is completed
   C. does not show human factors and informal working relationships
   D. is usually too complicated

24. The *span of control* for any supervisor is the
    A. number of tasks he is expected to perform himself
    B. amount of office space he and his subordinates occupy
    C. amount of work he is responsible for getting out
    D. number of subordinates he can supervise effectively

25. Of the following duties performed by a supervising employee, which would be considered a LINE function rather than a staff function?
    A. Evaluation of office personnel
    B. Recommendations for disciplinary action
    C. Initiating budget requests for replacement of equipment
    D. Inspections, at irregular times, of conditions and staff in the field

KEY (CORRECT ANSWERS)

1. C
2. D
3. C
4. A
5. A

6. C
7. B
8. A
9. A
10. C

11. B
12. A
13. D
14. C
15. B

16. C
17. B
18. A
19. B
20. C

21. B
22. A
23. C
24. D
25. D

PHILOSOPHY, PRINCIPLES, PRACTICES, AND TECHNICS
OF
SUPERVISION, ADMINISTRATION, MANAGEMENT, AND ORGANIZATION

CONTENTS

	Page
I. MEANING OF SUPERVISION	1
II. THE OLD AND THE NEW SUPERVISION	1
III. THE EIGHT (8) BASIC PRINCIPLES OF THE NEW SUPERVISION	1
1. Principle of Responsibility	1
2. Principle of Authority	1
3. Principle of Self-Growth	1
4. Principle of Individual Worth	2
5. Principle of Creative Leadership	2
6. Principle of Success and Failure	2
7. Principle of Science	2
8. Principle of Cooperation	2
IV. WHAT IS ADMINISTRATION?	3
1. Practices Commonly Classed as "Supervisory"	3
2. Practices Commonly Classed as "Administrative"	3
3. Practices Classified as Both "Supervisory" and "Administrative"	3
V. RESPONSIBILITIES OF THE SUPERVISOR	3
VI. COMPETENCIES OF THE SUPERVISOR	4
VII. THE PROFESSIONAL SUPERVISOR-EMPLOYEE RELATIONSHIP	4
VIII. MINI-TEXT IN SUPERVISION, ADMINISTRATION, MANAGEMENT, AND ORGANIZATION	5
A. Brief Highlights	
1. Levels of Management	5
2. What the Supervisor Must Learn	5
3. A Definition of Supervision	6
4. Elements of the Team Concept	6
5. Principles of Organization	6
6. The Four Important Parts of Every Job	6
7. Principles of Delegation	6
8. Principles of Effective Communications	6
9. Principles of Work Improvement	6
10. Areas of Job Improvement	7
11. Seven Key Points in Making Improvements	7
12. Corrective Techniques of Job Improvement	7
13. A Planning Checklist	7
14. Five Characteristics of Good Directions	7
15. Types of Directions	8
16. Controls	8
17. Orienting the New Employee	8
18. Checklist for Orienting New Employees	8
19. Principles of Learning	8
20. Causes of Poor Performance	8
21. Four Major Steps in On-The-Job Instructions	8

CONTENTS (cont'd)

	Page
22. Employees Want Five Things	9
23. Some Don'ts in Regard to Praise	9
24. How to Gain Your Workers' Confidence	9
25. Sources of Employee Problems	9
26. The Supervisor's Key to Discipline	9
27. Five Important Processes of Management	10
28. When the Supervisor Fails to Plan	10
29. Fourteen General Principles of Management	10
30. Change	10
B. Brief Topical Summaries	11
I. Who/What is the Supervisor?	11
II. The Sociology of Work	11
III. Principles and Practices of Supervision	11
IV. Dynamic Leadership	12
V. Processes for Solving Problems	12
VI. Training for Results	13
VII. Health, Safety, and Accident Prevention	13
VIII. Equal Employment Opportunity	13
IX. Improving Communications	14
X. Self-Development	14
XI. Teaching and Training	14
A. The Teaching Process	14
1. Preparation	15
2. Presentation	15
3. Summary	15
4. Application	15
5. Evaluation	15
B. Teaching Methods	15
1. Lecture	16
2. Discussion	16
3. Demonstration	16
4. Performance	16
5. Which Method to Use	16

PHILOSOPHY, PRINCIPLES, PRACTICES, AND TECHNICS
OF
SUPERVISION, ADMINISTRATION, MANAGEMENT, AND ORGANIZATION

I. MEANING OF SUPERVISION

The extension of the democratic philosophy has been accompanied by an extension in the scope of supervision. Modern leaders and supervisors no longer think of supervision in the narrow sense of being confined chiefly to visiting employees, supplying materials, or rating the staff. They regard supervision as being intimately related to all the concerned agencies of society, they speak of the supervisor's function in terms of "growth", rather than the "improvement," of employees

This modern concept of supervision may be defined as follows:

Supervision is leadership and the development of leadership within groups which are cooperatively engaged in inspection, research, training, guidance and evaluation.

II. THE OLD AND THE NEW SUPERVISION

TRADITIONAL	MODERN
1. Inspection	1. Study and analysis
2. Focused on the employee	2. Focused on aims, materials, methods, supervisors, employees, environment
3. Visitation	3. Demonstrations, intervisitation, workshops, directed reading, bulletins, etc.
4. Random and haphazard	4. Definitely organized and planned (scientific)
5. Imposed and authoritarian	5. Cooperative and democratic
6. One person usually	6. Many persons involved (creative)

III. THE EIGHT (8) BASIC PRINCIPLES OF THE NEW SUPERVISION

1. *PRINCIPLE OF RESPONSIBILITY*

   Authority to act and responsibility for acting must be joined.
   a. If you give responsibility, give authority.
   b. Define employee duties clearly.
   c. Protect employees from criticism by others.
   d. Recognize the rights as well as obligations of employees.
   e. Achieve the aims of a democratic society insofar as it is possible within the area of your work.
   f. Establish a situation favorable to training and learning.
   g. Accept ultimate responsibility for everything done in your section, unit, office, division, department.
   h. Good administration and good supervision are inseparable.

2. *PRINCIPLE OF AUTHORITY*

   The success of the supervisor is measured by the extent to which the power of authority is not used.
   a. Exercise simplicity and informality in supervision.
   b. Use the simplest machinery of supervision.
   c. If it is good for the organization as a whole, it is probably justified.
   d. Seldom be arbitrary or authoritative.
   e. Do not base your work on the power of position or of personality.
   f. Permit and encourage the free expression of opinions.

3. *PRINCIPLE OF SELF-GROWTH*

   The success of the supervisor is measured by the extent to which, and the speed with which, he is no longer needed.
   a. Base criticism on principles, not on specifics.
   b. Point out higher activities to employees.

       c. Train for self-thinking by employees, to meet new situations.
       d. Stimulate initiative, self-reliance and individual responsibility.
       e. Concentrate on stimulating the growth of employees rather than on removing defects.
4. *PRINCIPLE OF INDIVIDUAL WORTH*
    Respect for the individual is a paramount consideration in supervision.
       a. Be human and sympathetic in dealing with employees.
       b. Don't nag about things to be done.
       c. Recognize the individual differences among employees and seek opportunities to permit best expression of each personality.
5. *PRINCIPLE OF CREATIVE LEADERSHIP*
    The best supervision is that which is not apparent to the employee.
       a. Stimulate, don't drive employees to creative action.
       b. Emphasize doing good things.
       c. Encourage employees to do what they do best.
       d. Do not be too greatly concerned with details of subject or method.
       e. Do not be concerned exclusively with immediate problems and activities.
       f. Reveal higher activities and make them both desired and maximally possible.
       g. Determine procedures in the light of each situation but see that these are derived from a sound basic philosophy.
       h. Aid, inspire and lead so as to liberate the creative spirit latent in all good employees.
6. *PRINCIPLE OF SUCCESS AND FAILURE*
    There are no unsuccessful employees, only unsuccessful supervisors who have failed to give proper leadership.
       a. Adapt suggestions to the capacities, attitudes, and prejudices of employees.
       b. Be gradual, be progressive, be persistent.
       c. Help the employee find the general principle; have the employee apply his own problem to the general principle.
       d. Give adequate appreciation for good work and honest effort.
       e. Anticipate employee difficulties and help to prevent them.
       f. Encourage employees to do the desirable things they will do anyway.
       g. Judge your supervision by the results it secures.
7. *PRINCIPLE OF SCIENCE*
    Successful supervision is scientific, objective, and experimental. It is based on facts, not on prejudices.
       a. Be cumulative in results.
       b. Never divorce your suggestions from the goals of training.
       c. Don't be impatient of results.
       d. Keep all matters on a professional, not a personal level.
       e. Do not be concerned exclusively with immediate problems and activities.
       f. Use objective means of determining achievement and rating where possible.
8. *PRINCIPLE OF COOPERATION*
    Supervision is a cooperative enterprise between supervisor and employee.
       a. Begin with conditions as they are.
       b. Ask opinions of all involved when formulating policies.

  c. Organization is as good as its weakest link.
  d. Let employees help to determine policies and department programs.
  e. Be approachable and accessible - physically and mentally.
  f. Develop pleasant social relationships.

IV. WHAT IS ADMINISTRATION?

Administration is concerned with providing the environment, the material facilities, and the operational procedures that will promote the maximum growth and development of supervisors and employees. (Organization is an aspect, and a concomitant, of administration.)

There is no sharp line of demarcation between supervision and administration; these functions are intimately interrelated and, often, overlapping. They are complementary activities.

1. *PRACTICES COMMONLY CLASSED AS "SUPERVISORY"*
   a. Conducting employees conferences
   b. Visiting sections, units, offices, divisions, departments
   c. Arranging for demonstrations
   d. Examining plans
   e. Suggesting professional reading
   f. Interpreting bulletins
   g. Recommending in-service training courses
   h. Encouraging experimentation
   i. Appraising employee morale
   j. Providing for intervisitation

2. *PRACTICES COMMONLY CLASSIFIED AS "ADMINISTRATIVE"*
   a. Management of the office
   b. Arrangement of schedules for extra duties
   c. Assignment of rooms or areas
   d. Distribution of supplies
   e. Keeping records and reports
   f. Care of audio-visual materials
   g. Keeping inventory records
   h. Checking record cards and books
   i. Programming special activities
   j. Checking on the attendance and punctuality of employees

3. *PRACTICES COMMONLY CLASSIFIED AS BOTH "SUPERVISORY" AND "ADMINISTRATIVE"*
   a. Program construction
   b. Testing or evaluating outcomes
   c. Personnel accounting
   d. Ordering instructional materials

V. RESPONSIBILITIES OF THE SUPERVISOR

A person employed in a supervisory capacity must constantly be able to improve his own efficiency and ability. He represents the employer to the employees and only continuous self-examination can make him a capable supervisor.

Leadership and training are the supervisor's responsibility. An efficient working unit is one in which the employees work with the supervisor. It is his job to bring out the best in his employees. He must always be relaxed, courteous and calm in his association with his employees. Their feelings are important, and a harsh attitude does not develop the most efficient employees.

VI. COMPETENCIES OF THE SUPERVISOR
1. Complete knowledge of the duties and responsibilities of his position.
2. To be able to organize a job, plan ahead and carry through.
3. To have self-confidence and initiative.
4. To be able to handle the unexpected situation and make quick decisions.
5. To be able to properly train subordinates in the positions they are best suited for.
6. To be able to keep good human relations among his subordinates.
7. To be able to keep good human relations between his subordinates and himself and to earn their respect and trust.

VII. THE PROFESSIONAL SUPERVISOR-EMPLOYEE RELATIONSHIP

There are two kinds of efficiency: one kind is only apparent and is produced in organizations through the exercise of mere discipline; this is but a simulation of the second, or true, efficiency which springs from spontaneous cooperation. If you are a manager, no matter how great or small your responsibility, it is your job, in the final analysis, to create and develop this involuntary cooperation among the people whom you supervise. For, no matter how powerful a combination of money, machines, and materials a company may have, this is a dead and sterile thing without a team of willing, thinking and articulate people to guide it.

The following 21 points are presented as indicative of the exemplary basic relationship that should exist between supervisor and employee:

1. Each person wants to be liked and respected by his fellow employee and wants to be treated with consideration and respect by his superior.
2. The most competent employee will make an error. However, in a unit where good relations exist between the supervisor and his employees, tenseness and fear do not exist. Thus, errors are not hidden or covered up and the efficiency of a unit is not impaired.
3. Subordinates resent rules, regulations, or orders that are unreasonable or unexplained.
4. Subordinates are quick to resent unfairness, harshness, injustices and favoritism.
5. An employee will accept responsibility if he knows that he will be complimented for a job well done, and not too harshly chastized for failure; that his supervisor will check the cause of the failure, and, if it was the supervisor's fault, he will assume the blame therefor. If it was the employee's fault, his supervisor will explain the correct method or means of handling the responsibility.
6. An employee wants to receive credit for a suggestion he has made, that is used. If a suggestion cannot be used, the employee is entitled to an explanation. The supervisor should not say "no" and close the subject.
7. Fear and worry slow up a worker's ability. Poor working environment can impair his physical and mental health. A good supervisor avoids forceful methods, threats and arguments to get a job done.
8. A forceful supervisor is able to train his employees individually and as a team, and is able to motivate them in the proper channels.

9. A mature supervisor is able to properly evaluate his subordinates and to keep them happy and satisfied.
10. A sensitive supervisor will never patronize his subordinates.
11. A worthy supervisor will respect his employees' confidences.
12. Definite and clear-cut responsibilities should be assigned to each executive.
13. Responsibility should always be coupled with corresponding authority.
14. No change should be made in the scope or responsibilities of a position without a definite understanding to that effect on the part of all persons concerned.
15. No executive or employee, occupying a single position in the organization, should be subject to definite orders from more than one source.
16. Orders should never be given to subordinates over the head of a responsible executive. Rather than do this, the officer in question should be supplanted.
17. Criticisms of subordinates should, whever possible, be made privately, and in no case should a subordinate be criticized in the presence of executives or employees of equal or lower rank.
18. No dispute or difference between executives or employees as to authority or responsibilities should be considered too trivial for prompt and careful adjudication.
19. Promotions, wage changes, and disciplinary action should always be approved by the executive immediately superior to the one directly responsible.
20. No executive or employee should ever be required, or expected, to be at the same time an assistant to, and critic of, another.
21. Any executive whose work is subject to regular inspection should, whever practicable, be given the assistance and facilities necessary to enable him to maintain an independent check of the quality of his work.

VIII. MINI-TEXT IN SUPERVISION, ADMINISTRATION, MANAGEMENT, AND ORGANIZATION
A. BRIEF HIGHLIGHTS
Listed concisely and sequentially are major headings and important data in the field for quick recall and review.
1. *LEVELS OF MANAGEMENT*

   Any organization of some size has several levels of management. In terms of a ladder the levels are:

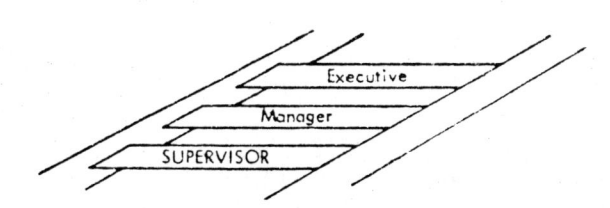

   Executive
   Manager
   SUPERVISOR

   The first level is very important because it is the beginning point of management leadership.
2. *WHAT THE SUPERVISOR MUST LEARN*

   A supervisor must learn to:
   (1) Deal with people and their differences
   (2) Get the job done through people
   (3) Recognize the problems when they exist
   (4) Overcome obstacles to good performance
   (5) Evaluate the performance of people
   (6) Check his own performance in terms of accomplishment

3. *A DEFINITION OF SUPERVISOR*
   The term supervisor means any individual having authority, in the interests of the employer, to hire, transfer, suspend, lay-off, recall, promote, discharge, assign, reward, or discipline other employees... or responsibility to direct them, or to adjust their grievances, or effectively to recommend such action, if, in connection with the foregoing, exercise of such authority is not of a merely routine or clerical nature but requires the use of independent judgment.

4. *ELEMENTS OF THE TEAM CONCEPT*
   What is involved in teamwork? The component parts are:
   (1) Members   (3) Goals   (5) Cooperation
   (2) A leader   (4) Plans   (6) Spirit

5. *PRINCIPLES OF ORGANIZATION*
   (1) A team member must know what his job is
   (2) Be sure that the nature and scope of a job are understood
   (3) Authority and responsibility should be carefully spelled out
   (4) A supervisor should be permitted to make the maximum number of decisions affecting his employees
   (5) Employees should report to only one supervisor
   (6) A supervisor should direct only as many employees as he can handle effectively
   (7) An organization plan should be flexible
   (8) Inspection and performance of work should be separate
   (9) Organizational problems should receive immediate attention
   (10) Assign work in line with ability and experience

6. *THE FOUR IMPORTANT PARTS OF EVERY JOB*
   (1) Inherent in every job is the *accountability* for results
   (2) A second set of factors in every job are *responsibilities*
   (3) Along with duties and responsibilities one must have the *authority* to act within certain limits without obtaining permission to proceed
   (4) No job exists in a vacuum. The supervisor is surrounded by key *relationships*

7. *PRINCIPLES OF DELEGATION*
   Where work is delegated for the first time, the supervisor should think in terms of these questions:
   (1) Who is best qualified to do this?
   (2) Can an employee improve his abilities by doing this?
   (3) How long should an employee spend on this?
   (4) Are there any special problems for which he will need guidance?
   (5) How broad a delegation can I make?

8. *PRINCIPLES OF EFFECTIVE COMMUNICATIONS*
   (1) Determine the media
   (2) To whom directed?
   (3) Identification and source authority
   (4) Is communication understood?

9. *PRINCIPLES OF WORK IMPROVEMENT*
   (1) Most people usually do only the work which is assigned to them
   (2) Workers are likely to fit assigned work into the time available to perform it
   (3) A good workload usually stimulates output
   (4) People usually do their best work when they know that results will be reviewed or inspected

(5) Employees usually feel that someone else is responsible for conditions of work, workplace layout, job methods, type of tools and equipment, and other such factors
(6) Employees are usually defensive about their job security
(7) Employees have natural resistance to change
(8) Employees can support or destroy a supervisor
(9) A supervisor usually earns the respect of his people through his personal example of diligence and efficiency

10. *AREAS OF JOB IMPROVEMENT*
The *areas* of job improvement are quite numerous, but the most common ones which a supervisor can identify and utilize are:
    (1) Departmental layout   (5) Work methods
    (2) Flow of work   (6) Materials handling
    (3) Workplace layout   (7) Utilization
    (4) Utilization of manpower   (8) Motion economy

11. *SEVEN KEY POINTS IN MAKING IMPROVEMENTS*
    (1) Select the job to be improved
    (2) Study how it is being done now
    (3) Question the present method
    (4) Determine actions to be taken
    (5) Chart proposed method
    (6) Get approval and apply
    (7) Solicit worker participation

12. *CORRECTIVE TECHNIQUES OF JOB IMPROVEMENT*

Specific Problems	*General Problems*	*Corrective Technique*
(1) Size of workload	(1) Departmental layout	(1) Study with scale model
(2) Inability to meet schedules	(2) Flow of work	(2) Flow chart study
(3) Strain and fatigue	(3) Workplan layout	(3) Motion analysis
(4) Improper use of men and skills	(4) Utilization of manpower	(4) Comparison of units produced to standard allowances
(5) Waste, poor quality, unsafe conditions	(5) Work methods	(5) Methods analysis
(6) Bottleneck conditions that hinder output	(6) Materials handling	(6) Flow chart and equipment study
(7) Poor utilization of equipment and machines	(7) Utilization of equipment	(7) Down time vs. running time
(8) Efficiency and productivity of labor	(8) Motion economy	(8) Motion analysis

13. *A PLANNING CHECKLIST*
    (1) Objectives   (8) Equipment
    (2) Controls   (9) Supplies and materials
    (3) Delegations   (10) Utilization of time
    (4) Communications   (11) Safety
    (5) Resources   (12) Money
    (6) Methods and procedures (13) Work
    (7) Manpower   (14) Timing of improvements

14. *FIVE CHARACTERISTICS OF GOOD DIRECTIONS*
In order to get results, directions must be:
    (1) Possible of accomplishment   (4) Planned and complete
    (2) Agreeable with worker interests (5) Unmistakably clear
    (3) Related to mission

15. *TYPES OF DIRECTIONS*
    (1) Demands or direct orders   (3) Suggestion or implication
    (2) Requests   (4) Volunteering
16. *CONTROLS*
    A typical listing of the overall areas in which the supervisor should establish controls might be:
    (1) Manpower   (4) Quantity of work   (7) Money
    (2) Materials   (5) Time   (8) Methods
    (3) Quality of work (6) Space
17. *ORIENTING THE NEW EMPLOYEE*
    (1) Prepare for him   (3) Orientation for the job
    (2) Welcome the new employee   (4) Follow-up
18. *CHECKLIST FOR ORIENTING NEW EMPLOYEES*
                                                                    Yes No
    (1) Do your appreciate the feelings of new employees when they first report for work? ... ...
    (2) Are you aware of the fact that the new employee must make a big adjustment to his job? ... ...
    (3) Have you given him good reasons for liking the job and the organization? ... ...
    (4) Have you prepared for his first day on the job? ... ...
    (5) Did you welcome him cordially and make him feel needed? ... ...
    (6) Did you establish rapport with him so that he feels free to talk and discuss matters with you? ... ...
    (7) Did you explain his job to him and his relationship to you? ... ...
    (8) Does he know that his work will be evaluated periodically on a basis that is fair and objective? ... ...
    (9) Did you introduce him to his fellow workers in such a way that they are likely to accept him? ... ...
    (10) Does he know what employee benefits he will receive? ... ...
    (11) Does he understand the importance of being on the job and what to do if he must leave his duty station? ... ...
    (12) Has he been impressed with the importance of accident prevention and safe practice? ... ...
    (13) Does he generally know his way around the department? ... ...
    (14) Is he under the guidance of a sponsor who will teach the right ways of doing things? ... ...
    (15) Do you plan to follow-up so that he will continue to adjust successfully to his job? ... ...
19. *PRINCIPLES OF LEARNING*
    (1) Motivation   (2) Demonstration or explanation
    (3) Practice
20. *CAUSES OF POOR PERFORMANCE*
    (1) Improper training for job   (6) Lack of standards of
    (2) Wrong tools   performance
    (3) Inadequate directions   (7) Wrong work habits
    (4) Lack of supervisory follow-up (8) Low morale
    (5) Poor communications   (9) Other
21. *FOUR MAJOR STEPS IN ON-THE-JOB INSTRUCTION*
    (1) Prepare the worker   (3) Tryout performance
    (2) Present the operation   (4) Follow-up

22. *EMPLOYEES WANT FIVE THINGS*
    (1) Security   (2) Opportunity   (3) Recognition
    (4) Inclusion (5) Expression
23. *SOME DON'TS IN REGARD TO PRAISE*
    (1) Don't praise a person for something he hasn't done
    (2) Don't praise a person unless you can be sincere
    (3) Don't be sparing in praise just because your superior withholds it from you
    (4) Don't let too much time elapse between good performance and recognition of it
24. *HOW TO GAIN YOUR WORKERS' CONFIDENCE*
    Methods of developing confidence include such things as:
    (1) Knowing the interests, habits, hobbies of employees
    (2) Admitting your own inadequacies
    (3) Sharing and telling of confidence in others
    (4) Supporting people when they are in trouble
    (5) Delegating matters that can be well handled
    (6) Being frank and straightforward about problems and working conditions
    (7) Encouraging others to bring their problems to you
    (8) Taking action on problems which impede worker progress
25. *SOURCES OF EMPLOYEE PROBLEMS*
    On-the-job causes might be such things as:
    (1) A feeling that favoritism is exercised in assignments
    (2) Assignment of overtime
    (3) An undue amount of supervision
    (4) Changing methods or systems
    (5) Stealing of ideas or trade secrets
    (6) Lack of interest in job
    (7) Threat of reduction in force
    (8) Ignorance or lack of communications
    (9) Poor equipment
    (10) Lack of knowing how supervisor feels toward employee
    (11) Shift assignments
    Off-the-job problems might have to do with:
    (1) Health   (2) Finances   (3) Housing   (4) Family
26. *THE SUPERVISOR'S KEY TO DISCIPLINE*
    There are several key points about discipline which the supervisor should keep in mind:
    (1) Job discipline is one of the disciplines of life and is directed by the supervisor.
    (2) It is more important to correct an employee fault than to fix blame for it.
    (3) Employee performance is affected by problems both on the job and off.
    (4) Sudden or abrupt changes in behavior can be indications of important employee problems.
    (5) Problems should be dealt with as soon as possible after they are identified.
    (6) The attitude of the supervisor may have more to do with solving problems than the techniques of problem solving.
    (7) Correction of employee behavior should be resorted to only after the supervisor is sure that training or counseling will not be helpful
    (8) Be sure to document your disciplinary actions.

(9) Make sure that you are disciplining on the basis of facts rather than personal feelings.
(10) Take each disciplinary step in order, being careful not to make snap judgments, or decisions based on impatience.

27. *FIVE IMPORTANT PROCESSES OF MANAGEMENT*
    (1) Planning   (2) Organizing   (3) Scheduling
    (4) Controlling   (5) Motivating

28. *WHEN THE SUPERVISOR FAILS TO PLAN*
    (1) Supervisor creates impression of not knowing his job
    (2) May lead to excessive overtime
    (3) Job runs itself-- supervisor lacks control
    (4) Deadlines and appointments missed
    (5) Parts of the work go undone
    (6) Work interrupted by emergencies
    (7) Sets a bad example
    (8) Uneven workload creates peaks and valleys
    (9) Too much time on minor details at expense of more important tasks

29. *FOURTEEN GENERAL PRINCIPLES OF MANAGEMENT*
    (1) Division of work   (8) Centralization
    (2) Authority and responsibility   (9) Scalar chain
    (3) Discipline   (10) Order
    (4) Unity of command   (11) Equity
    (5) Unity of direction   (12) Stability of tenure of personnel
    (6) Subordination of individual interest to general interest
    (13) Initiative
    (7) Remuneration of personnel   (14) Esprit de corps

30. *CHANGE*
Bringing about change is perhaps attempted more often, and yet less well understood, than anything else the supervisor does. How do people generally react to change? (People tend to resist change that is imposed upon them by other individuals or circumstances.)

Change is characteristic of every situation. It is a part of every real endeavor where the efforts of people are concerned.

  A. Why do people resist change?
    People may resist change because of:
    (1) Fear of the unknown
    (2) Implied criticism
    (3) Unpleasant experiences in the past
    (4) Fear of loss of status
    (5) Threat to the ego
    (6) Fear of loss of economic stability

  B. How can we best overcome the resistance to change?
    In initiating change, take these steps:
    (1) Get ready to sell
    (2) identify sources of help
    (3) Anticipate objections
    (4) Sell benefits
    (5) Listen in depth
    (6) Follow up

B. BRIEF TOPICAL SUMMARIES

I. WHO/WHAT IS THE SUPERVISOR?
1. The supervisor is often called the "highest level employee and the lowest level manager."
2. A supervisor is a member of both management and the work group. He acts as a bridge between the two.
3. Most problems in supervision are in the area of human relations, or people problems.
4. Employees expect: Respect, opportunity to learn and to advance, and a sense of belonging, and so forth.
5. Supervisors are responsible for directing people and organizing work. Planning is of paramount importance.
6. A position description is a set of duties and responsibilities inherent to a given position.
7. It is important to keep the position description up-to-date and to provide each employee with his own copy.

II. THE SOCIOLOGY OF WORK
1. People are alike in many ways; however each individual is unique.
2. The supervisor is challenged in getting to know employee differences. Acquiring skills in evaluating individuals is an asset.
3. Maintaining meaningful working relationships in the organization is of great importance.
4. The supervisor has an obligation to help individuals to develop to their fullest potential.
5. Job rotation on a planned basis helps to build versatility and to maintain interest and enthusiasm in work groups.
6. Cross training (job rotation) provides backup skills.
7. The supervisor can help reduce tension by maintaining a sense of humor, providing guidance to employees, and by making reasonable and timely decisions. Employees respond favorably to working under reasonably predictable circumstances.
8. Change is characteristic of all managerial behavior. The supervisor must adjust to changes in procedures, new methods, technological changes, and to a number of new and sometimes challenging situations.
9. To overcome the natural tendency for people to resist change, the supervisor should become more skillful in initiating change.

III. PRINCIPLES AND PRACTICES OF SUPERVISION
1. Employees should be required to answer to only one superior.
2. A supervisor can effectively direct only a limited number of employees, depending upon the complexity, variety, and proximity of the jobs involved.
3. The organizational chart presents the organization in graphic form. It reflects lines of authority and responsibility as well as interrelationships of units within the organization.
4. Distribution of work can be improved through an analysis using the "Work Distribution Chart."
5. The "Work Distribution Chart" reflects the division of work within a unit in understandable form.
6. When related tasks are given to an employee, he has a better chance of increasing his skills through training.
7. The individual who is given the responsibility for tasks must also be given the appropriate authority to insure adequate results.
8. The supervisor should delegate repetitive, routine work. Preparation of recurring reports, maintaining leave and attendance records are some examples.

9. Good discipline is essential to good task performance. Discipline is reflected in the actions of employees on the job in the absence of supervision.
10. Disciplinary action may have to be taken when the positive aspects of discipline have failed. Reprimand, warning, and suspension are examples of disciplinary action.
11. If a situation calls for a reprimand, be sure it is deserved and remember it is to be done in private.

IV. DYNAMIC LEADERSHIP
1. A style is a personal method or manner of exerting influence.
2. Authoritarian leaders often see themselves as the source of power and authority.
3. The democratic leader often perceives the group as the source of authority and power.
4. Supervisors tend to do better when using the pattern of leadership that is most natural for them.
5. Social scientists suggest that the effective supervisor use the leadership style that best fits the problem or circumstances involved.
6. All four styles -- telling, selling, consulting, joining -- have their place. Using one does not preclude using the other at another time.
7. The theory X point of view assumes that the average person dislikes work, will avoid it whenever possible, and must be coerced to achieve organizational objectives.
8. The theory Y point of view assumes that the average person considers work to be as natural as play, and, when the individual is committed, he requires little supervision or direction to accomplish desired objectives.
9. The leader's basic assumptions concerning human behavior and human nature affect his actions, decisions, and other managerial practices.
10. Dissatisfaction among employees is often present, but difficult to isolate. The supervisor should seek to weaken dissatisfaction by keeping promises, being sincere and considerate, keeping employees informed, and so forth.
11. Constructive suggestions should be encouraged during the natural progress of the work.

V. PROCESSES FOR SOLVING PROBLEMS
1. People find their daily tasks more meaningful and satisfying when they can improve them.
2. The causes of problems, or the key factors, are often hidden in the background. Ability to solve problems often involves the ability to isolate them from their backgrounds. There is some substance to the cliché that some persons "can't see the forest for the trees."
3. New procedures are often developed from old ones. Problems should be broken down into manageable parts. New ideas can be adapted from old ones.
4. People think differently in problem-solving situations. Using a logical, patterned approach is often useful. One approach found to be useful includes these steps:
   (a) Define the problem   (d) Weigh and decide
   (b) Establish objectives (e) Take action
   (c) Get the facts   (f) Evaluate action

VI. TRAINING FOR RESULTS
1. Participants respond best when they feel training is important to them.
2. The supervisor has responsibility for the training and development of those who report to him.
3. When training is delegated to others, great care must be exercised to insure the trainer has knowledge, aptitude, and interest for his work as a trainer.
4. Training (learning) of some type goes on continually. The most successful supervisor makes certain the learning contributes in a productive manner to operational goals.
5. New employees are particularly susceptible to training. Older employees facing new job situations require specific training, as well as having need for development and growth opportunities.
6. Training needs require continuous monitoring.
7. The training officer of an agency is a professional with a responsibility to assist supervisors in solving training problems.
8. Many of the self-development steps important to the supervisor's own growth are equally important to the development of peers and subordinates. Knowledge of these is important when the supervisor consults with others on development and growth opportunities.

VII. HEALTH, SAFETY, AND ACCIDENT PREVENTION
1. Management-minded supervisors take appropriate measures to assist employees in maintaining health and in assuring safe practices in the work environment.
2. Effective safety training and practices help to avoid injury and accidents.
3. Safety should be a management goal. All infractions of safety which are observed should be corrected without exception.
4. Employees' safety attitude, training and instruction, provision of safe tools and equipment, supervision, and leadership are considered highly important factors which contribute to safety and which can be influenced directly by supervisors.
5. When accidents do occur they should be investigated promptly for very important reasons, including the fact that information which is gained can be used to prevent accidents in the future.

VIII. EQUAL EMPLOYMENT OPPORTUNITY
1. The supervisor should endeavor to treat all employees fairly, without regard to religion, race, sex, or national origin.
2. Groups tend to reflect the attitude of the leader. Prejudice can be detected even in very subtle form. Supervisors must strive to create a feeling of mutual respect and confidence in every employee.
3. Complete utilization of all human resources is a national goal. Equitable consideration should be accorded women in the work force, minority-group members, the physically and mentally handicapped, and the older employee. The important question is: "Who can do the job?"
4. Training opportunities, recognition for performance, overtime assignments, promotional opportunities, and all other personnel actions are to be handled on an equitable basis.

IX. IMPROVING COMMUNICATIONS

1. Communications is achieving understanding between the sender and the receiver of a message. It also means sharing information -- the creation of understanding.
2. Communication is basic to all human activity. Words are means of conveying meanings; however, real meanings are in people.
3. There are very practical differences in the effectiveness of one-way, impersonal, and two-way communications. Words spoken face-to-face are better understood. Telephone conversations are effective, but lack the rapport of person-to-person exchanges. The whole person communicates.
4. Cooperation and communication in an organization go hand-in-hand. When there is a mutual respect between people, spelling out rules and procedures for communicating is unnecessary.
5. There are several barriers to effective communications. These include failure to listen with respect and understanding, lack of skill in feedback, and misinterpreting the meanings of words used by the speaker. It is also common practice to listen to what we want to hear, and tune out things we do not want to hear.
6. Communication is management's chief problem. The supervisor should accept the challenge to communicate more effectively and to improve interagency and intra-agency communications.
7. The supervisor may often plan for and conduct meetings. The planning phase is critical and may determine the success or the failure of a meeting.
8. Speaking before groups usually requires extra effort. Stage fright may never disappear completely, but it can be controlled.

X. SELF-DEVELOPMENT

1. Every employee is responsible for his own self-development.
2. Toastmaster and toastmistress clubs offer opportunities to improve skills in oral communications.
3. Planning for one's own self-development is of vital importance. Supervisors know their own strengths and limitations better than anyone else.
4. Many opportunities are open to aid the supervisor in his developmental efforts, including job assignments; training opportunities, both governmental and non-governmental -- to include universities and professional conferences and seminars.
5. Programmed instruction offers a means of studying at one's own rate.
6. Where difficulties may arise from a supervisor's being away from his work for training, he may participate in televised home study or correspondence courses to meet his self-development needs.

XI. TEACHING AND TRAINING

A. The Teaching Process

Teaching is encouraging and guiding the learning activities of students toward established goals. In most cases this process consists in five steps: preparation, presentation, summarization, evaluation, and application.

1. Preparation
    Preparation is twofold in nature; that of the supervisor and the employee.
    Preparation by the supervisor is absolutely essential to success. He must know what, when, where, how, and whom he will teach. Some of the factors that should be considered are:
    (1) The objectives   (5) Employee interest
    (2) The materials needed (6) Training aids
    (3) The methods to be used (7) Evaluation
    (4) Employee participation (8) Summarization
    Employee preparation consists in preparing the employee to receive the material. Probably the most important single factor in the preparation of the employee is arousing and maintaining his interest. He must know the objectives of the training, why he is there, how the material can be used, and its importance to him.
2. Presentation
    In presentation, have a carefully designed plan and follow it. The plan should be accurate and complete, yet flexible enough to meet situations as they arise. The method of presentation will be determined by the particular situation and objectives.
3. Summary
    A summary should be made at the end of every training unit and program. In addition, there may be internal summaries depending on the nature of the material being taught. The important thing is that the trainee must always be able to understand how each part of the new material relates to the whole.
4. Application
    The supervisor must arrange work so the employee will be given a chance to apply new knowledge or skills while the material is still clear in his mind and interest is high. The trainee does not really know whether he has learned the material until he has been given a chance to apply it. If the material is not applied, it loses most of its value.
5. Evaluation
    The purpose of all training is to promote learning. To determine whether the training has been a success or failure, the supervisor must evaluate this learning.
    In the broadest sense evaluation includes all the devices, methods, skills, and techniques used by the supervisor to keep himself and the employees informed as to their progress toward the objectives they are pursuing. The extent to which the employee has mastered the knowledge, skills, and abilities, or changed his attitudes, as determined by the program objectives, is the extent to which instruction has succeeded or failed.
    Evaluation should not be confined to the end of the lesson, day, or program but should be used continuously. We shall note later the way this relates to the rest of the teaching process.

B. Teaching Methods
    A teaching method is a pattern of identifiable student and instructor activity used in presenting training material.
    All supervisors are faced with the problem of deciding which method should be used at a given time.

1. Lecture
    The lecture is direct oral presentation of material by the supervisor. The present trend is to place less emphasis on the trainer's activity and more on that of the trainee.
2. Discussion
    Teaching by discussion or conference involves using questions and other techniques to arouse interest and focus attention upon certain areas, and by doing so creating a learning situation. This can be one of the most valuable methods because it gives the employees an opportunity to express their ideas and pool their knowledge.
3. Demonstration
    The demonstration is used to teach how something works or how to do something. It can be used to show a principle or what the results of a series of actions will be. A well-staged demonstration is particularly effective because it shows proper methods of performance in a realistic manner.
4. Performance
    Performance is one of the most fundamental of all learning techniques or teaching methods. The trainee may be able to tell how a specific operation should be performed but he cannot be sure he knows how to perform the operation until he has done so.

As with all methods, there are certain advantages and disadvantages to each method.

5. Which Method to Use
    Moreover, there are other methods and techniques of teaching. It is difficult to use any method without other methods entering into it. In any learning situation a combination of methods is usually more effective than any one method alone.

Finally, evaluation must be integrated into the other aspects of the teaching-learning process.

It must be used in the motivation of the trainees; it must be used to assist in developing understanding during the training; and it must be related to employee application of the results of training.

This is distinctly the role of the supervisor.

BASIC FUNDAMENTALS OF OCCUPATIONAL SAFETY AND HEALTH ORGANIZATION

Analysis of safety and health programs in organizations or companies with outstanding records shows that invariably the most successful programs are built around these seven elements:

I. MANAGEMENT LEADERSHIP
    Responsibility
    Policy

II. ASSIGNMENT OF AUTHORITY
    Safety and Health Directors
    Safety and Health Committees
    Small Plant Organizations
    Scattered Operations

III. MAINTENANCE OF SAFE AND HEALTHFUL WORKING CONDITIONS
    Inspection of Work Areas
    Fire Inspections
    Health Surveys
    Job Safety Analysis

IV. ESTABLISHMENT OF SAFETY AND HEALTH TRAINING
    Employee
    Supervisor
    Job Instruction Training

V. ACCIDENT RECORD/DATA COLLECTION SYSTEM
    Records
    Accident Investigation
    Accident Analysis
    Rates
    Countermeasures

VI. HEALTH, MEDICAL AND FIRST AID SYSTEMS
    Health
    Medical
    First Aid

VII. ACCEPTANCE OF PERSONAL ACCOUNTABILITY BY EMPLOYEES
    Maintaining Interest

These seven elements of accident prevention are the same in any industry regardless of the operation and in any establishment or plant, large or small.

I. MANAGEMENT LEADERSHIP

Responsibility

Top management's attitude toward accident prevention in any company or business is almost invariably reflected in the attitude of the supervisory force. Similarly, the employees' attitude is usually the same as the supervisors'. Thus, if the top executive is not genuinely interested in preventing accidents, injuries, and occupational illnesses, no one else is likely to be. Since this basic fact applies to every level of management and supervision, an accident prevention program must have top management's personal commitment and a demonstrated interest if employee cooperation and participation are to be obtained.

Policy

To initiate the program, top management must issue a clear-cut statement of policy for the guidance of middle management, supervisors, and employees. Such a statement of policy will indicate top management's viewpoint in principle, and should cover in general the basic elements.

The details for carrying out an accident prevention program may be assigned, but the responsibility for the basic policy cannot be delegated.

Concern for the safety and health of a firm's employees doesn't stop here but also requires its active interest and participation in all of the major elements of the safety and health organization.

II. ASSIGNMENT OF AUTHORITY

Safety and Health Directors

Safety activities, like any other phase of business, must have leadership and guidance. It is of paramount importance that management assign the authority to direct the safety and health program to one individual. The individual must be formally trained, or the training must be provided on the job in the field of occupational safety and health. The title may be the safety and health director or engineer, the safety manager, or the safety supervisor, depending upon the organization, the nature of the duties assigned, and the personal qualifications. While the occupational safety and health director's exact role varies, the job usually covers:

- Developing and implementing a safety and health program.
- Identifying and controlling hazards.
- Advising management on conformance with company policy and government safety regulations.
- Helping employees understand their safety responsibilities and practices (working through the first line supervisor).
- Evaluating the severity and causes of accidents.
- Evaluating the effectiveness of the safety and health program and improving it where necessary.

To fulfill these responsibilities, persons responsible for safety and health need to maintain direct contact with line and staff supervision.

The first-line supervisor is a key person in the accident prevention program. To the worker, the supervisor is management, because this is the management level that is closest to the people. The supervisor is also the prime communicator with employees on safety and health matters.

With guidance and help from the safety and health director, first-line supervisors should:

- Establish safe work practices and conditions.
- Enforce safety rules.
- Teach employees how to recognize hazards.
- Report all injuries and assure prompt treatment.
- Investigate the causes of all accidents and see that action to prevent recurrence is completed.

Accident prevention efforts and results should be included in the supervisor's performance evaluations.

Safety and Health Committees

Safety and health committees are found in almost every successful organization.

In union plants, joint labor-management safety and health committees are established in accordance with the labor agreement.

An efficient, smoothly operating committee is one in which management and employees are in agreement as to the limit of their duties and responsibilities. Also, labor and management must make every effort to carry out their obligations.

The committee organization will vary from plant to plant and from time to time. Much depends upon the size of the organization, the type of problems, and the smoothness and character of employee relations.

The basic function of a safety and health committee is to create and maintain an active interest in safety and health and to reduce accidents and occupational illnesses. The following duties are examples of those sometimes assigned to safety and health committees:

- Make a systematic inspection to discover and report potential health and safety hazards.
- Observe safety practices and procedures of the workforce.
- Review accident reports and corrective measures.
- Attempt to contribute a positive attitude toward safety and health.
- Listen to employees' concerns about safety and health matters.

Small Plant Organization

Active management and control of the small plant safety and health program may be vested in the chief executive, general manager, or in an experienced and qualified supervisor who has both authority and status.

There are several advantages inherent in small-scale operations, such as closer contact with the working force, more general acquaintance with the problems of the whole plant, and, frequently, less labor turnover. However, it may be difficult to justify a full-time safety and health professional, physician, nurse, or other medical services.

Scattered Operations

Organizations with operations in scattered locations and that require relatively few employees, such as some construction projects, face special inherent problems of organization. Their operations may be seasonal or intermittent and there may not be a sufficiently stable working force to operate committees effectively. The local manager, therefore, needs to adapt the safety and health program to the local conditions.

III. MAINTENANCE OF SAFE AND HEALTHY WORKING CONDITIONS

Inspection of Work Areas

Inspection of work areas can locate hazards and potential hazards which can adversely affect safety and health. Safety inspections are one of the principal means of locating accident sources. Removal of these hazards can lead to substantially improved accident prevention. In promptly correcting work conditions, management demonstrates to the employees its interest and sincerity in accident prevention.

Safety inspections should not be conducted primarily to find how many things are wrong, but rather to determine if everything is satisfactory. The whole purpose should be one of helpfulness in discovering conditions which, if corrected, will bring the plant up to accepted and approved standards.

It is advisable to schedule periodic inspections for the entire facility. Equipment or operations which present the greatest hazards should be inspected more frequently. Such inspections may be made monthly, semi-annually, annually, or at other suitable intervals. Some types of equipment, such as elevators, boilers, unfired pressure vessels, and fire extinguishing equipment, are required by law to be inspected at specific, regular intervals. Chains, cables, ropes, and other equipment subject to severe strain in handling heavy materials should be inspected at specified intervals. A careful record should be kept of each inspection.

Fire Inspections

One of the hazards having the greatest effect on an industrial plant is fire. Consequently, a system should be set up for periodic inspections of all types of fire protective equipment. Such inspections should include water tanks, sprinkler systems, standpipes, hose, fire plugs, extinguishers, and all other equipment used for fire protection. The schedule of inspections should be closely followed and an accurate record maintained.

Health Surveys

Whenever there is a suspected health hazard, a special inspection should be made to determine the extent of the hazard and the precautions or mechanical safeguarding needed to provide and maintain safe conditions. The services of an industrial hygienist may be needed. Physical examinations should be made of employees exposed to occupational health hazards.

Job Safety Analysis

Job safety analysis (JSA) is a procedure used to review job practices and uncover hazards that may be present. It is one of the first steps in hazard and accident analysis and in safety training. Supervisors and employees in completing the JSA learn more about the job. Study of the JSA will suggest ways for improvement of the job methods, resulting in better work procedures and fewer accidents. A JSA is often kept near a machine so that an operator can review it at any time, especially when starting a new job.

IV. ESTABLISHMENT OF SAFETY AND HEALTH TRAINING

Employees

Effective safety training for all employees is an essential part of any successful accident and illness prevention program. New employees need primary safety orientation to provide a base for future attitude development. They should be taught the specific work practices necessary for their jobs. Job hazards should be identified and proper controls and procedures explained. In beginning on a job, the new employee must be given adequate supervision to assure that the new employee gets started safely.

Supervisors

Supervisors must be trained in all areas of their safety responsibilities, such as hazard identification, job safety analysis, job instruction training, accident investigations, and human relations. Training must be updated whenever processes or operations change. Subjects for training should be related to accident experience.

Job Instruction Training

Job instruction training (JIT), the procedure for teaching a person how to perform a particular job, is accepted as one of the teaching tools in a quality instruction program.

V. ACCIDENT RECORD/DATA COLLECTION SYSTEM

Good recordkeeping is the foundation of a sound approach to occupational safety and health.

Records

Records of accidents and injuries are essential to efficient and successful safety programs, just as records of production, costs, sales, and profits and losses, are essential to the efficient and successful operation of a business. Records supply the information necessary to transform haphazard, costly, ineffective safety work into a planned safety program that controls both conditions and costs.

It is legally required that the company keep proper accident/illness records. It is highly desirable to establish a system for recording all accidents, not just those involving injuries. What may cause a property-damage-only accident today can be the cause of tomorrow's serious-injury accident.

To reduce the possibility of serious complications following a minor accident, there should be a system for reporting all injuries, no matter how trivial, so that prompt first aid treatment can be given and the accident investigated.

Accident Investigation

It is obvious that every accident that occurs should be thoroughly investigated as soon as possible to find its cause and to prevent a recurrence. In addition to accident prevention, other benefits include cost reduction (both the direct and the more sizable indirect costs), continuation of operations or activities without disruption, and the maintenance of good employee morale with its frequently realized higher productivity and fewer work problems.

The important record is the accident investigation report. Every accident should be thoroughly investigated by the immediate supervisor, or depending on its severity, by an accident fact-finding committee appointed by top management.

During the investigation, special inspection of the accident scene is essential. The accident investigation identifies what action should be taken and what improvements are needed to prevent similar accidents occurring in the future. It also documents the facts for use in instances of compensation and litigation.

Accident Analysis

Analyzing accident records will provide convenient and systematized warning. Causal data should be available from the accident report, including such items as the type of injury and body part; general cause, such as unsafe act and/or unsafe conditions; and specific causes such as caught in, contact with, fall from, overexertion, struck by, or struck against. This detail should be analyzed and preventive countermeasures developed.

In the United States, injury and occupational illness records are required by the Occupational Safety and Health Act and specific record requirements are published by OSHA.

Injuries and illnesses are recorded separately, with three different categories, as follows:

1. FATALITIES, regardless of the time between the injury and death, or the length of the illness;

2. LOST WORKDAY CASES, other than fatalities, that result in lost workdays;

3. NONFATAL CASES WITHOUT LOST WORKDAYS, which result in transfer to another job or termination of employment, or require medical treatment, or involve loss of consciousness or restriction of work or motion. This category also includes any diagnosed occupational illnesses that are reported to the employer, but are not classified as fatalities or lost workday cases.

Rates

Incidence rates, which relate the total number of injuries and illnesses per category to total employee-hours worked, can be computed from the formula:

$$\frac{\text{Number of injuries and illnesses} \times 200{,}000}{\text{Total hours worked by all employees during the period}}$$

The resulting rate will be expressed as incidents per 100 employees. These rates can be computed by operation within the plant to determine those areas with the most injuries. They can be used to detect incident rate trends within the plant. They can be used to compare your plant with similar plants or your industry.

Countermeasures

Once the accident and/or health hazard(s) has been identified and evaluated, then corrective action must be taken. In general, and in order of effectiveness, the items below should be considered.

- Change the system or machines, method, process, etc., to eliminate the hazard.
- Control the hazard by enclosing, guarding, etc.
- Train employees to increase awareness and to follow safe job procedures.
- Prescribe approved personal protection equipment, etc.

VI. HEALTH, MEDICAL, AND FIRST AID SYSTEMS.

Health Services

Occupational health services deal with both the person and the work environment. A comprehensive health program requires (a) concern with all aspects of the work environment that may harm an individual, and (b) a constructive approach to industrial production problems through medical supervision of the employee's health.

The program should be supervised by a physician interested in industrial employees and qualified in industrial medicine. To be effective, the program needs certain medical and first aid facilities, a necessary staff, and the full cooperation of management.

Medical

Preplacement examinations should be conducted to determine and record the physical condition of the prospective worker so that the employee can be assigned to a suitable job. The individual capabilities should meet or exceed the job requirements. Safety must be a factor in the "employee-job fit." Periodic examinations of all employees are sometimes necessary.

First Aid

First aid is an important part of a safety and health program. Immediate, temporary treatment by a qualified individual should be available in the case of accident or sudden illness before the services of a physician can be secured (if they are needed).

VII. ACCEPTANCE OF PERSONAL ACCOUNTABILITY BY EMPLOYEE

Employees make many contributions to the accident prevention programs through the safety suggestions they make and the safety activities in which they participate. But above all, each employee must be trained to work safely and to accept responsibility for his or her own safe work practices. A high degree of employee pride should be developed in the safety record along with the motivation to maintain and improve that record.

To be effective, a program for maintaining interest in safety and health must be based on employee needs. Such activities as contests, drawings, family affairs and award presentations, and the like, serve to reinforce and communicate the safety and health program to the employees. Safety and health programs are a continuing activity, not a one-shot project.

SUMMARY

Successful safety and health programs have distinguishing characteristics. These include:

1. Strong management commitment to safety and health that is shown by various actions reflecting management's support and involvement in activities.

2. Close contact and interaction between workers, supervisors and management enabling open communications on safety and health as well as other job-related matters.

3. Training practices emphasizing early indoctrination and followup instruction in job-safety procedures.

4. Evidence of added features of variations in conventional safety and health practices serving to enhance their effectiveness.

SAFETY IN CONFINED SPACES

INTRODUCTION

If you are required to construct or work in a:

BOILER, CUPOLA, DEGREASER, FURNACE, PIPELINE, PIT, PUMPING STATION, REACTION OR PROCESS VESSEL, SEPTIC TANK, SEWAGE DIGESTER, SEWER, SILO, STORAGE TANK, SHIP'S HOLD, UTILITY VAULT, VAT, or similar type enclosure,

you are working in a confined space (See examples on page 3).

How Can You Identify a Confined Space?

A confined space is a space which has any one of the following characteristics:

- limited openings for entry and exit

- unfavorable natural ventilation

- not designed for continuous worker occupancy.

Limited openings for entry and exit:
Confined space openings are limited primarily by size or location. Openings are usually small in size, perhaps as small as 18 inches in diameter, and are difficult to move through easily. Small openings may make it very difficult to get needed equipment in or out of the spaces, especially protective equipment such as respirators needed for entry into spaces with hazardous atmospheres, or life-saving equipment when rescue is needed. However, in some cases openings may be very large, for example open-topped spaces such as pits, degreasers, excavations, and ships' holds. Access to open-topped spaces may require the use of ladders, hoists, or other devices, and escape from such areas may be very difficult in emergency situations.

Unfavorable natural ventilation:
Because air may not move in and out of confined spaces freely due to the design, the atmosphere inside a confined space can be very different from the atmosphere outside. Deadly gases may be trapped inside, particularly if the space is used to store or process chemicals or organic substances which may decompose. There may not be enough oxygen inside the confined space to support life, or the air could be so oxygen-rich that it is likely to increase the chance of fire or explosion if a source of ignition is present.

Not designed for continuous worker occupancy:
Most confined spaces are not designed for workers to enter and work in them on a routine basis. They are designed to store a product, enclose materials and processes, or transport products or substances. Therefore, occasional worker entry for inspection, maintenance, repair, cleanup, or similar tasks is often difficult and dangerous due to chemical or physical hazards within the space.

A confined space found in the workplace may have a combination of these three characteristics, which can complicate working in and around these spaces as well as rescue operations during emergencies. If a survey of your working area identifies one or more work spaces with the characteristics listed above, **READ THE FOLLOWING INFORMATION - SOMEDAY IT MAY SAVE YOUR LIFE, OR THE LIFE OF A CO-WORKER.**

Storage Tank

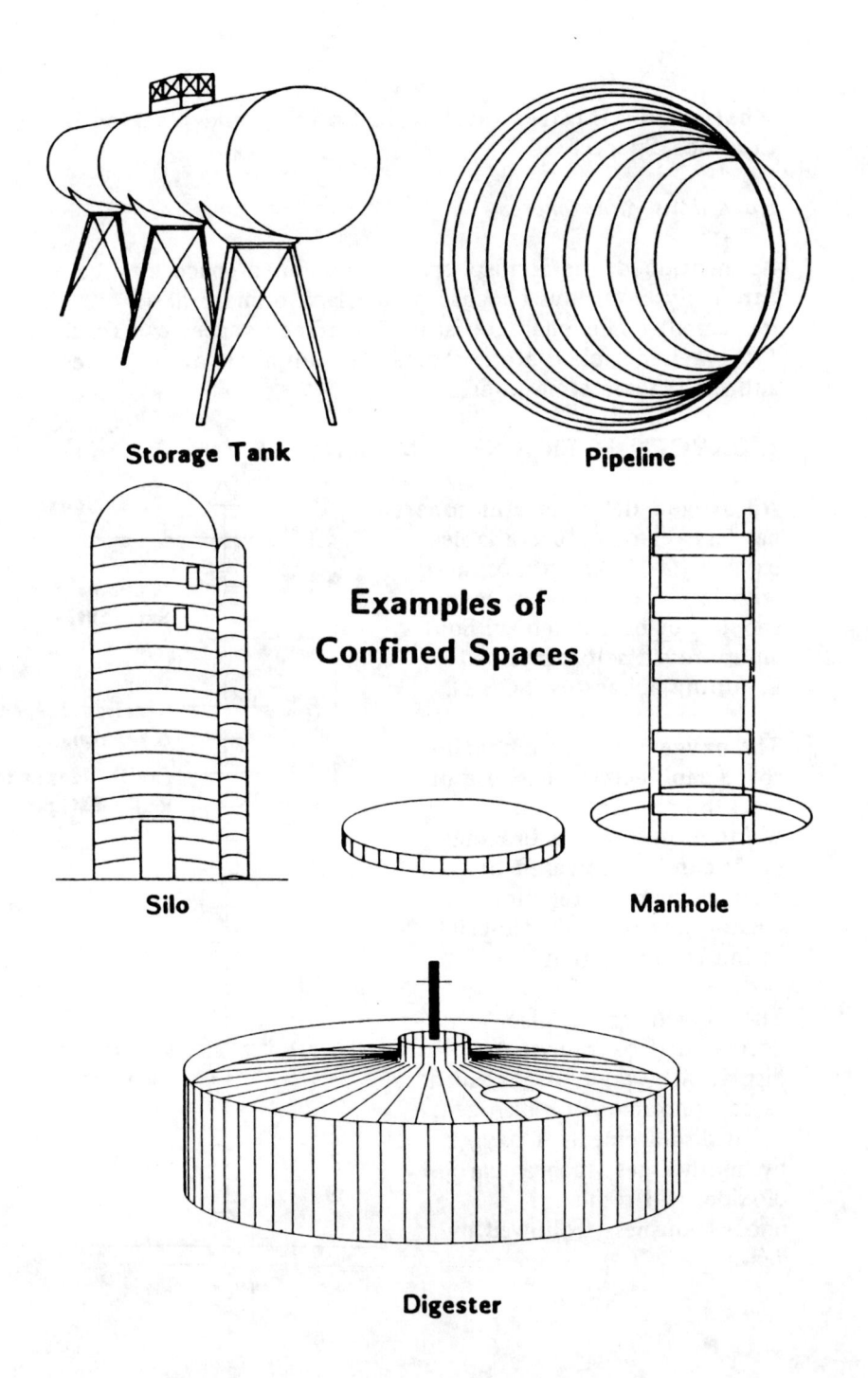

Pipeline

Examples of Confined Spaces

Silo

Manhole

Digester

-3-

What are the Hazards Involved in Entering and Working in Confined Spaces?

Hazardous Atmospheres

As mentioned, the atmosphere in a confined space may be extremely hazardous because of the lack of natural air movement. This characteristic of confined spaces can result in 1) oxygen-deficient atmospheres, 2) flammable atmospheres, and/or 3) toxic atmospheres.

1. OXYGEN-DEFICIENT ATMOSPHERES:

An oxygen-deficient atmosphere has less than 19.5% available oxygen (O_2). Any atmosphere with less than 19.5% oxygen should <u>not</u> be entered without an approved self-contained breathing apparatus (SCBA).

The oxygen level in a confined space can decrease because of work being done, such as welding, cutting, or brazing; or, it can be decreased by certain chemical reactions (rusting) or through bacterial action (fermentation).

The oxygen level is also decreased if oxygen is displaced by another gas, such as carbon dioxide or nitrogen. Total displacement of oxygen by another gas, such as carbon dioxide, will result in unconsciousness, followed by death.

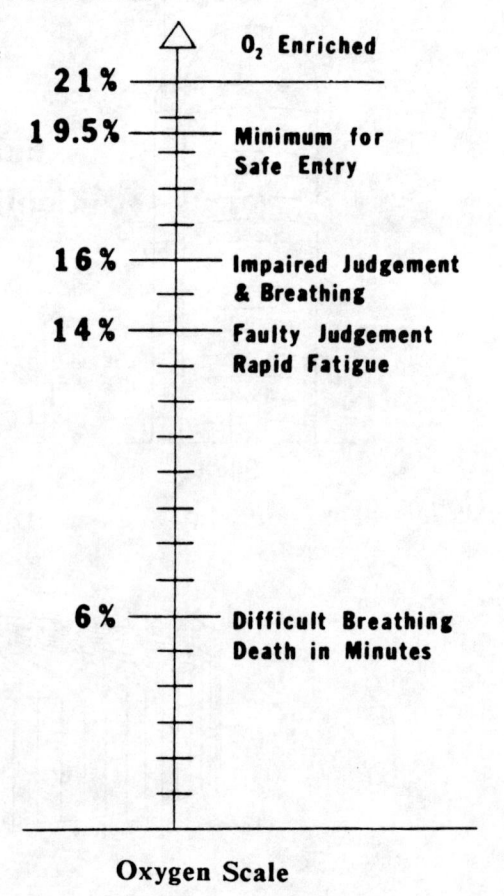

Oxygen %	Effect
21%	O_2 Enriched
19.5%	Minimum for Safe Entry
16%	Impaired Judgement & Breathing
14%	Faulty Judgement Rapid Fatigue
6%	Difficult Breathing Death in Minutes

Oxygen Scale

2. FLAMMABLE ATMOSPHERES:

Two things make an atmosphere flammable: 1) the oxygen in air; and 2) a flammable gas, vapor, or dust in the proper mixture. Different gases have different flammable ranges. If a source of ignition (e.g., a sparking or electrical tool) is introduced into a space containing a flammable atmosphere, an explosion will result.

An oxygen-enriched atmosphere (above 21%) will cause flammable materials, such as clothing and hair, to burn violently when ignited. Therefore, never use pure oxygen to ventilate a confined space. Ventilate with normal air.

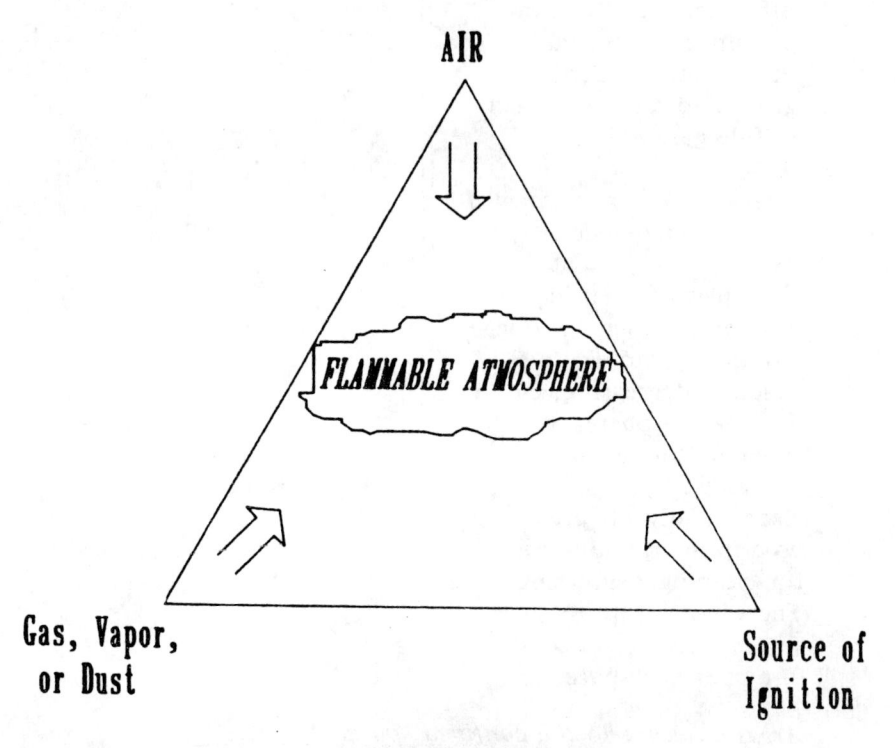

The Ignition Triangle

(AIR — Gas, Vapor, or Dust — Source of Ignition → FLAMMABLE ATMOSPHERE)

3. TOXIC ATMOSPHERES:

Most substances (liquids, vapors, gases, mists, solid materials, and dusts) should be considered hazardous in a confined space. Toxic substances can come from the following:

- *The product stored in the space:*

    The product can be absorbed into the walls and give off toxic gases when removed or when cleaning out the residue of a stored product, toxic gases can be given off. Example: Removal of sludge from a tank - decomposed material can give off deadly hydrogen sulfide gas.

- *The work being performed in a confined space:*

    Examples of such include welding, cutting, brazing, painting, scraping, sanding, degreasing, etc. Toxic atmospheres are generated in various processes. For example, cleaning solvents are used in many industries for cleaning/degreasing. The vapors from these solvents are very toxic in a confined space.

- *Areas adjacent to the confined space:*

    Toxicants produced by work in the <u>area</u> of confined spaces can enter and accumulate in confined spaces.

-6-

TESTING THE ATMOSPHERE

It is important to understand that some gases or vapors are heavier than air and will settle to the bottom of a confined space. Also, some gases are lighter than air and will be found around the top of the confined space. Therefore, it is necessary to test all areas (top, middle, bottom) of a confined space with properly calibrated testing instruments to determine what gases are present. If testing reveals oxygen-deficiency, or the presence of toxic gases or vapors, the space must be ventilated and re-tested before workers enter. If ventilation is not possible and entry is necessary (for emergency rescue, for example), workers must have appropriate respiratory protection.

NEVER TRUST YOUR SENSES TO DETERMINE IF THE AIR IN A CONFINED SPACE IS SAFE! YOU CAN NOT SEE OR SMELL MANY TOXIC GASES AND VAPORS, NOR CAN YOU DETERMINE THE LEVEL OF OXYGEN PRESENT.

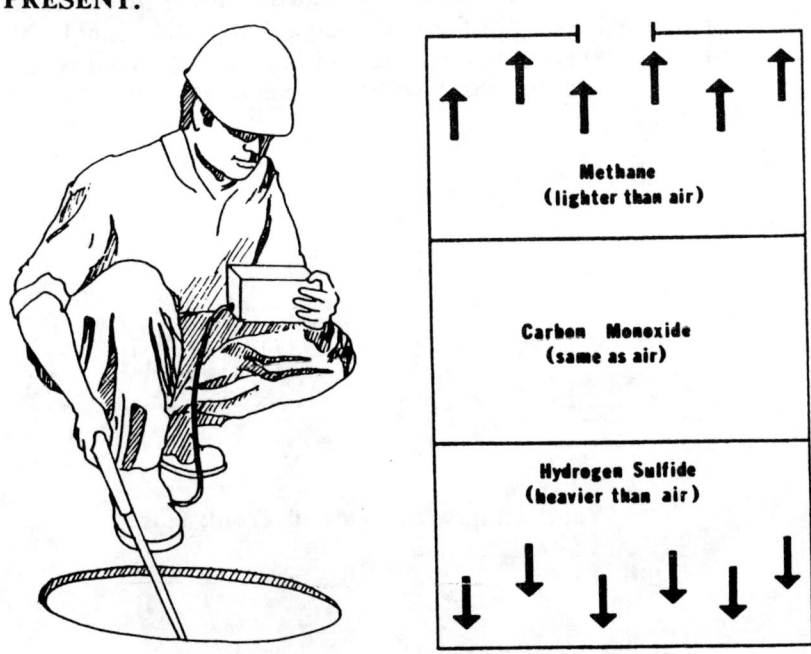

Methane (lighter than air)

Carbon Monoxide (same as air)

Hydrogen Sulfide (heavier than air)

From the Outside, Top to Bottom

-7-

VENTILATION

Ventilation by a blower or fan may be necessary to remove harmful gases and vapors from a confined space. There are several methods for ventilating a confined space. The method and equipment chosen are dependent upon the size of the confined space openings, the gases to be exhausted (e.g., are they flammable?), and the source of makeup air.

Under certain conditions where flammable gases or vapors have displaced the oxygen level, but are too rich to burn, forced air ventilation may dilute them until they are within the explosive range. Also, if inert gases (e.g. carbon dioxide, nitrogen, argon) are used in the confined space, the space should be well ventilated and re-tested before a worker may enter.

A common method of ventilation requires a large hose, one end attached to a fan and the other lowered into a manhole or opening. For example, a manhole would have the ventilating hose run to the bottom to blow out all harmful gases and vapors (see diagram). The air intake should be placed in an area that will draw in fresh air only. Ventilation should be continuous where possible, because in many confined spaces the hazardous atmosphere will form again when the flow of air is stopped.

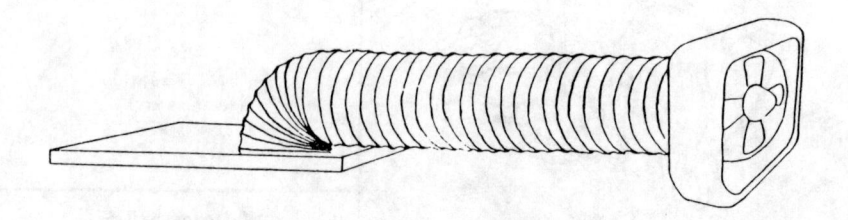

Ventilating with Fan and Trunk Hose

ISOLATION

Isolation of a confined space is a process where the space is removed from service by:

- *locking out*
  electrical sources, preferrably at disconnect switches remote from the equipment

- *blanking and bleeding*
  pneumatic and hydraulic lines

- *disconnecting*
  belt and chain drives, and mechanical linkages on shaft-driven equipment where possible, and

- *securing*
  mechanical moving parts within confined spaces with latches, chains, chocks, blocks, or other devices.

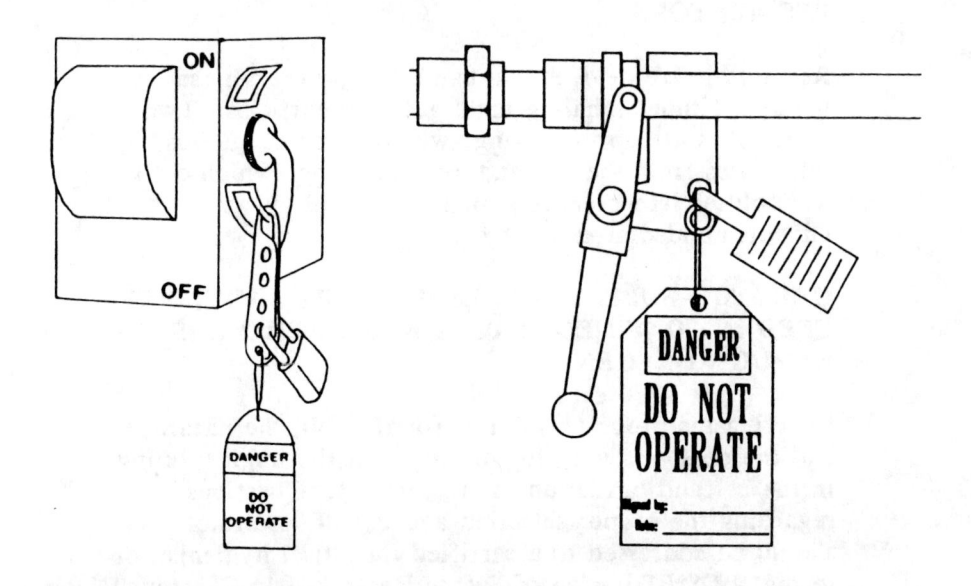

Examples of Lockout

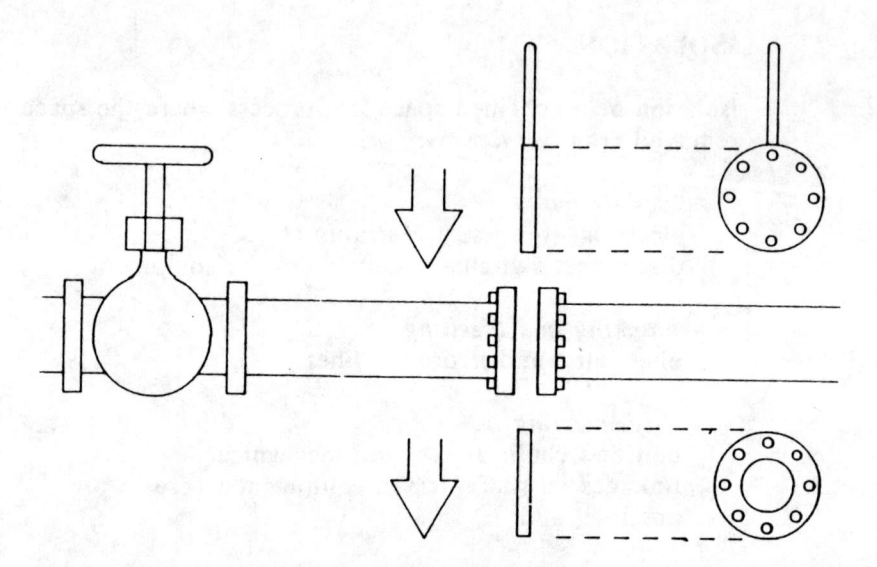

Method of Blanking Hydraulic/Pneumatic Lines

RESPIRATORS

Respirators are devices that can allow workers to safely breathe without inhaling toxic gases or particles. Two basic types are air-purifying, which filter dangerous substances from the air; and air-supplying, which deliver a supply of safe breathing air from a tank or an uncontaminated area nearby.

ONLY AIR-SUPPLYING RESPIRATORS SHOULD BE USED IN CONFINED SPACES WHERE THERE IS NOT ENOUGH OXYGEN.

Selecting the proper respirator for the job, the hazard, and the person is very important, as is thorough training in the use and limitations of respirators. Questions regarding the proper selection and use of respirators should be addressed to a certified industrial hygienist, or to the NIOSH Division of Safety Resarch, 944 Chestnut Ridge Rd., Morgantown, West Virginia 26505.

Air-Purifying Respirators

(Do Not Use in Oxygen-Deficient Atmosphere)

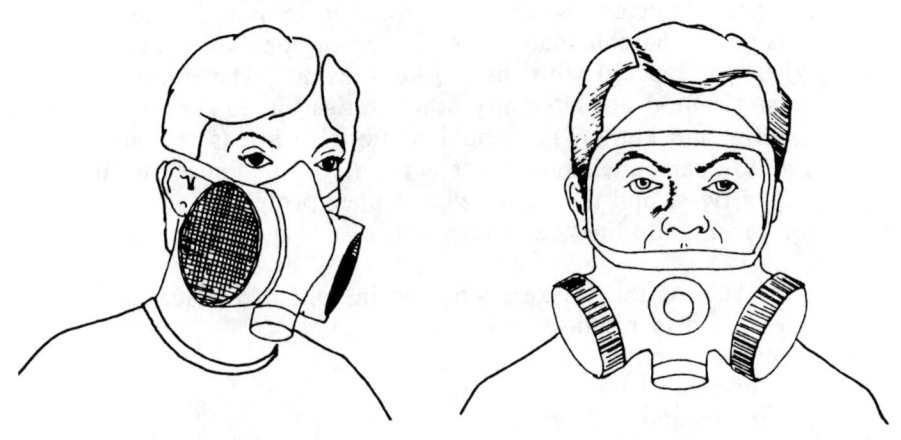

Half-mask   *Full-Facepiece*

Air-Supplying Respirators

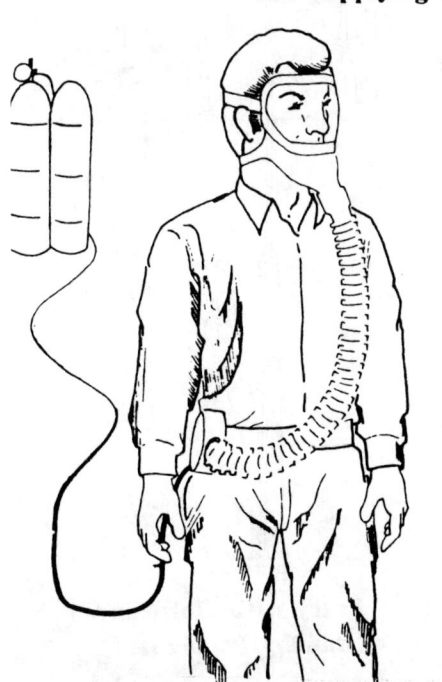

Supplied Air Respirator with Auxiliary, Escape-only SCBA

Self-contained Breathing Apparatus (SCBA)

STANDBY/RESCUE

A standby person should be assigned to remain on the outside of the confined space and be in constant contact (visual or speech) with the workers inside. The standby person should not have any other duties but to serve as standby and know who should be notified in case of emergency. Standby personnel should not enter a confined space until help arrives, and then only with proper protective equipment, life lines, and respirators.

Over 50% of the workers who die in confined spaces are attempting to rescue other workers. Rescuers must be trained in and follow established emergency procedures and use appropriate equipment and techniques (lifelines, respiratory protection, standby persons, etc.). Steps for safe rescue should be included in all confined space entry procedures. Rescue should be well planned and drills should be frequently conducted on emergency procedures. Unplanned rescue, such as when someone instinctively rushes in to help a downed co-worker, can easily result in a double fatality, or even multiple fatalities if there are more than one would-be rescuers.

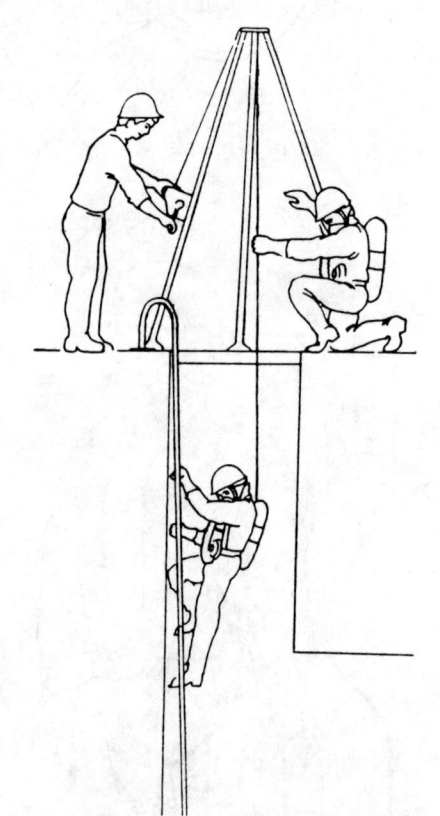

Entry with Hoist and Standby Personnel

REMEMBER: AN UNPLANNED RESCUE WILL PROBABLY BE YOUR <u>LAST</u>.

GENERAL/PHYSICAL HAZARDS

In addition to the areas discussed above, evaluation of a confined space should consider the following potential hazards:

1. TEMPERATURE EXTREMES:

   Extremely hot or cold temperatures can present problems for workers. For example, if the space has been steamed, it should be allowed to cool before any entry is made.

2. ENGULFMENT HAZARDS:

   Loose, granular material stored in bins and hoppers, such as grain, sand, coal, or similar material, can engulf and suffocate a worker. The loose material can crust or bridge over in a bin and break loose under the weight of a worker.

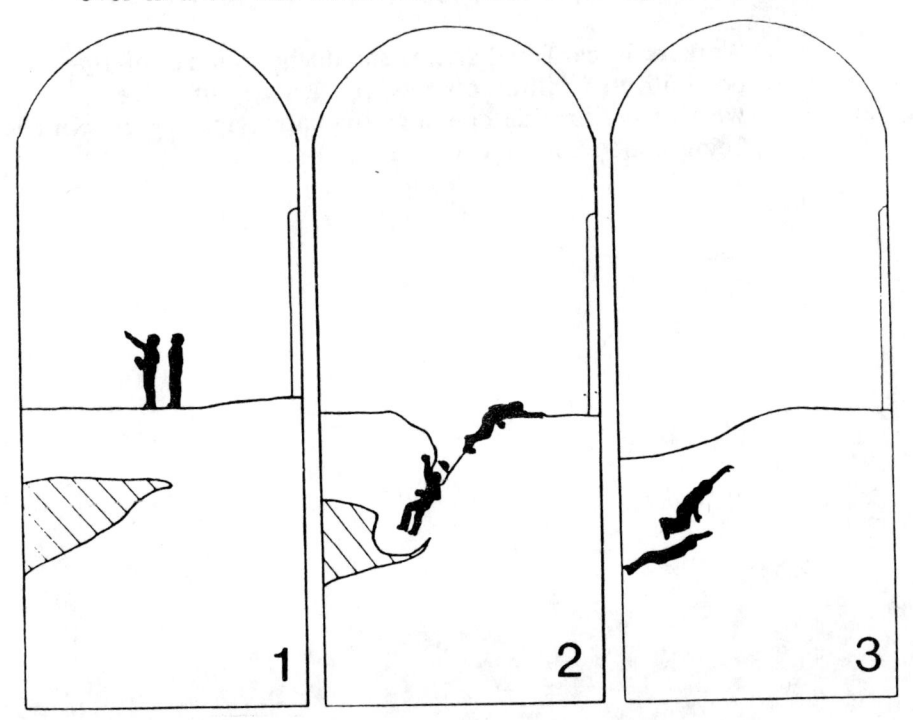

The Hazard of Engulfment in Unstable Material

3. NOISE:

Noise within a confined space can be amplified because of the design and acoustic properties of the space. Excessive noise can not only damage hearing, but can also affect communication, such as causing a shouted warning to go unheard.

4. SLICK/WET SURFACES:

Slips and falls can occur on a wet surface causing injury or death to workers. Also, a wet surface will increase the likelihood for and effect of electric shock in areas where electrical circuits, equipment, and tools are used.

5. FALLING OBJECTS:

Workers in confined spaces should be mindful of the possibility of falling objects, particularly in spaces which have topside openings for entry, and where work is being done above the worker.

RECOMMENDATIONS FOR SAFE ENTRY: A CHECKLIST

Use the following checklist to evaluate the confined space.

DO <u>NOT</u> ENTER A CONFINED SPACE UNTIL YOU HAVE CONSIDERED EVERY QUESTION, AND HAVE DETERMINED THE SPACE TO BE SAFE.

<u>YES NO</u>

☐ ☐ *Is entry necessary?*

TESTING

☐ ☐ *Are the instruments used in atmospheric testing properly calibrated?*

☐ ☐ *Was the atmosphere in the confined space tested?*

☐ ☐ *Was Oxygen at least 19.5% - not more than 21%?*

☐ ☐ *Were toxic, flammable, or oxygen-displacing gases/vapors present?*

   - Hydrogen Sulfide

   - Carbon Monoxide

   - Methane

   - Carbon Dioxide

   - Other (list) _____
   _____

YES NO

MONITORING

☐ ☐ *Will the atmosphere in the space be monitored while work is going on?*

☐ ☐ *Continuously?*

☐ ☐ *Periodically? (If yes, give interval: _____)*

REMEMBER - ATMOSPHERIC CHANGES OCCUR DUE TO THE WORK PROCEDURE OR THE PRODUCT STORED. THE ATMOSPHERE MAY BE SAFE WHEN YOU ENTER, BUT CAN CHANGE VERY QUICKLY.

CLEANING

☐ ☐ *Has the space been cleaned before entry is made?*

☐ ☐ *Was the space steamed?*

☐ ☐ *If so, was it allowed to cool?*

VENTILATION

☐ ☐ *Has the space been ventilated before entry?*

☐ ☐ *Will ventilation be continued during entry?*

☐ ☐ *Is the air intake for the ventilation system located in an area that is free of combustible dusts and vapors and toxic substances?*

☐ ☐ *If atmosphere was found unacceptable and then ventilated, was it re-tested before entry?*

<u>YES</u> <u>NO</u>

ISOLATION

☐ ☐ *Has the space been isolated from other systems?*

☐ ☐ *Has electrical equipment been locked out?*

☐ ☐ *Have disconnects been used where possible?*

☐ ☐ *Has mechanical equipment been blocked, chocked, and disengaged where necessary?*

☐ ☐ *Have lines under pressure been blanked and bled?*

CLOTHING/EQUIPMENT

☐ ☐ *Is special clothing required (boots, chemical suits, glasses, etc.)?*

    (If so, specify: _____)

☐ ☐ *Is special equipment required (e.g., rescue equipment, communications equipment, etc.)?*

    (If so, specify: _____)

☐ ☐ *Are special tools required (e.g., sparkproof)?*

    (If so, specify: _____)

RESPIRATORY PROTECTION

☐ ☐ *Are MSHA/NIOSH-approved respirators of the type required available at the worksite?*

☐ ☐ *Is respiratory protection required (e.g., air-purifying, supplied air, self-contained breathing apparatus, etc.)?*

    (If so, specify type: _____)

<u>YES</u> <u>NO</u>

☐ ☐ *Can you get through the opening with a respirator on? (If you don't know, find out before you try to enter.)*

TRAINING

☐ ☐ *Have you been trained in proper use of a respirator?*

☐ ☐ *Have you received first aid/CPR training?*

☐ ☐ *Have you been trained in confined space entry and do you know what to look for?*

STANDBY/RESCUE

☐ ☐ *Will there be a standby person on the outside in constant visual or auditory communication with the person on the inside?*

☐ ☐ *Will the standby person be able to see and/or hear the person inside at all times?*

☐ ☐ *Has the standby person(s) been trained in rescue procedures?*

☐ ☐ *Will safety lines and harness be required to remove a person?*

☐ ☐ *Are company rescue procedures available to be followed in the event of an emergency?*

☐ ☐ *Are you familiar with emergency rescue procedures?*

☐ ☐ *Do you know who to notify and how in the event of an emergency?*

YES NO

PERMIT

(The permit is an authorization in writing that states that the space has been tested by a qualified person, that the space is safe for entry; what precautions, equipment, etc. are required; and what work is to be done.)

☐ ☐ *Has a confined space entry permit been issued?*

☐ ☐ *Does the permit include a list of emergency telephone numbers?*

For further information on confined spaces, occupational hazards, safe work practices, and other topics which could affect your wellbeing, write to:

PUBLICATIONS DISSEMINATION
National Institute for Occupational
Safety and Health
Robert A. Taft Laboratories
4676 Columbia Parkway
Cincinnati, OH 45226

Lack of hazard awareness and unplanned rescue attempts led to the following deaths:

On July 23, 1985, a city worker was removing an inspection plate from a sewer line in a 50-foot deep pump station, when the plate blew off allowing raw sewage to enter the room. Two fellow workers and a policeman attempted to rescue the worker from the sludge filled room and were unsuccessful. All four were dead when removed from the pumping station.

On February 21, 1986, a self-employed truck driver died after entering the top of a 22-foot high x 15-foot square sawdust bin. He suffocated when the sawdust inside the bin collapsed and buried him.

On July 5, 1986, a worker entered a chemical degreaser tank to clean out the bottom and collapsed. Two fellow workers noticed the man down and went in to rescue him. All three workers died.

On July 16, 1986, a worker entered a septic tank to clean out the residue at the bottom and collapsed shortly afterward. Two workers on the outside went in to rescue the downed worker. All three were dead when removed from the tank.

On October 10, 1986, a self-employed plumbing contractor entered an underground water line vault to inspect a backflow device. The contractor collapsed shortly after entering the vault. A supervisor noticed the man down, and entered the vault in a rescue attempt. Both men had entered an untested oxygen-deficient atmosphere, and died as a result.

On February 6, 1987, two workers (father and son) at a wastewater plant were working on a digester that was being drained. They went on top of the digester and opened a hatch to check the sludge level. To provide light in the digester, they lowered an extension cord with an exposed 200 watt light bulb into the digester. The light broke and caused the methane gas in the digester to explode, killing both men instantly.

If the guidelines in this pamphlet had been followed, these fatalities would have been prevented.

ANSWER SHEET

TEST NO. _____ PART _____ TITLE OF POSITION _____
(AS GIVEN IN EXAMINATION ANNOUNCEMENT - INCLUDE OPTION, IF ANY)

PLACE OF EXAMINATION _____ DATE _____
(CITY OR TOWN)   (STATE)

RATING

USE THE SPECIAL PENCIL. MAKE GLOSSY BLACK MARKS.

Make only ONE mark for each answer. Additional and stray marks may be counted as mistakes. In making corrections, erase errors COMPLETELY.

ANSWER SHEET

NOV - - 2016

TEST NO. _____ PART ____ TITLE OF POSITION _____
(AS GIVEN IN EXAMINATION ANNOUNCEMENT - INCLUDE OPTION, IF ANY)

PLACE OF EXAMINATION _____ DATE _____
(CITY OR TOWN)   (STATE)

RATING

USE THE SPECIAL PENCIL.   MAKE GLOSSY BLACK MARKS.

Make only ONE mark for each answer.   Additional and stray marks may be counted as mistakes.   In making corrections, erase errors COMPLETELY.